HURRICANE PARTY & COMPANION PLAYS
BY DAVID THIGPEN

Hurricane Party
& Companion Plays

BY DAVID THIGPEN

edited by **Robert Z Grant**
and **Lisa Kicielinski**

THE COLLECTIVE NY

HURRICANE PARTY & COMPANION PLAYS, OCTOBER 2020

Copyright © 2020 by The Collective: Theatre, Arts & Film, Ltd.

Rights reserved. Published in the United States. New York, New York.

Permissions can be found at the end of the book.

Cataloging-in-Publication data is on file at the Library of Congress.

ISBN: 978-0-9911968-7-6

www.thecollective-ny.org

Printed in the United States of America
10 9 8 7 6 5 4 3

This play is dedicated to the members of The Collective NY, for fearlessly helping me find my voice. And to Josh Webb, for reminding me that no story comes from thin air.

CONTENTS

Hurricane Party began in 2017 as a series of long-form improvisations with The Collective NY, a company that incubates theatre, film and television in New York City. The ideas were inspired by a tradition from where I come from in South Carolina, where often during hurricane season, people hunker down together to ride out a weather event that can vary from mildly disruptive and underwhelming to catastrophic and deadly. The events in life that excite me the most and compel me to dramatize them are the ones where the temperature is up as far as it can go. Much of my work for the past several years has been rooted in the southeast, and I had a few key actors that I was in the groove of tailoring roles for, so the situation in the play seemed a natural fit to explore. Over the course of a year, scenes developed and eventually grew into a full-length play, not dissimilar from the one scripted here. By the end of that year, following a pair of fruitful readings, a production was scheduled for a fall run at The Cherry Lane Theatre in Manhattan in 2018.

My least favorite question to be asked about this play, or anything I write, is: "What are you trying to say?" While I have great admiration and respect for writers whose stories are inspired by philosophical or social aim, operating from that place does not instinctually occur to me. I tend to start work aiming a lens at a dark place with seemingly grotesque characters whose world may seem foreign and whose actions may seem unreasonable at first. Over the course of the play, we begin to find a common ground with these people that we didn't see possible, and to discover a relationship with them as texturally real as our own personal ones. While these characteristics may not lead us toward an academic summation of the play, hopefully they ignite realizations that are both painfully true and full of beauty for their truth.

In rehearsals for Hurricane Party, director Maria Dizzia, who displayed more graceful patience and insight than I realized possible, told me that the play is about "saying goodbye to a world we no longer belong to." I believe that. In spite of the story's cruelty and darkness, it presents a world of people fighting passionately for love and not wanting to let go. Seeing that as the play's fulcrum will be important for anyone attempting this play.

The period of time from that first improv all the way to this publication amplified the power of shared creative process for me. The play may be "the thing," but everything around it makes it theatre. That feels particularly true as I write this in summer of 2020: With every day's growing uncertainty, imagining a world with a room — where we can all gather, tell a story, and be vulnerable enough to see ourselves in everyone around us — seems more important than ever.

HURRICANE PARTY & COMPANION PLAYS
BY DAVID THIGPEN

Hurricane Party
by David Thigpen

HURRICANE PARTY by David Thigpen was first produced at The Cherry Lane Theatre in New York City, and premiered September 11, 2018. It was directed by Maria Dizzia. Stage Manager was Bianca Puorto. The cast (in order of appearance) was as follows:

MACON	Sayra Player
DANA	Kevin Kane
TODD	Michael Abbott Jr.
CAROLINE	Booker Garrett
TABBY	Lacy Marie Meyer
JADE	Toni Lachelle Pollitt

SETTING
Conway, South Carolina

TIME
Now

SCENE 1

(From the dark we hear two people fucking. A light in the room grows to reveal her riding him. She's MACON. He's DANA.)

MACON: Ah hunh.

DANA: Ohhhh. Okay—

MACON: Ohhhh yeah! Right there. Right there! Shit, shit, shit...God!

DANA: Okay...God!

MACON: God! FUCK. ME.

DANA: Wait, wait, wait—

MACON: Don't quit! Git it! Fuck me!

(He flips her over and climbs on top.)

MACON: Back in! Put it back in!

DANA: Okay—

MACON: Whoa! Ohp. Little higher!

DANA: Sorry—

MACON: Nice try—

DANA: I didn't mean to—I wasn't tryin' to—

MACON: We're good. Just shut up and fuck me! Shut up and fuuuuuuuck! *(Stacatto.)* Git me daddy, git me daddy, git me daddy—

DANA: Y'alright?

MACON: DON'T. STOP.

(They climax. They catch their breath. She goes for a cigarette.)

DANA: Imma be sore.

MACON: Yer gonna be sore. That's funny. Scratch m'back.

(He does.)

MACON: Over there. Good. Mmm. Do one of those things, "X marks the spot, question mark, dot dot dot, slot slot— *(Notices the time.)* OHHH shit. We gotta get up and at 'em—

DANA: I swear— *(Slides on his boxers and tidies up the wreckage.)*

MACON: Yer so good. Lookit you. Wobblin' like a baby giraffe.

(He stumbles. She giggles. He tosses her some shorts. They stare at each other.)

MACON: Goddamn.

DANA: What's on yer mind, Macon?

MACON: Can't believe it's you.

DANA : Me what?

MACON: That you—Come here.

(He does. She wraps her arms around him. Kiss.)

MACON: Those eyes.

DANA: What? I got hamster eyes.

MACON: No you don't.

DANA: I do, I do, I do.

(They kiss deep. Long.)

DANA: You been standin' here years and yer still like nothin' I ever seen.

MACON; Y'make my stomach drop down and back up through my throat.

DANA: Yeah?

MACON: Yes sir.

DANA: Right here?

MACON: Over there.

☾

DANA: It's not here—

MACON: Don't do it—

DANA: Do what?

MACON: No!

(He pins her to the bed and goes wild tickling her. She loses control.)

MACON: Yer gonna make me pee everywhere!

(He relents. She makes a break for the kitchen.)

DANA: Y'all find that dog yet?

MACON: No sir. I'm guessin' he found that highway before crossin' the rainbow bridge.

DANA: Cryin' ass shame.

(She laughs.)

DANA: Nah fer real. I love Taco. He was my favorite.

MACON: *(Eats an old cheeseburger from the kitchen counter.)* All we do is look for him.

DANA: Gimme a bite.

MACON: Ha. No. Magic word?

DANA: Please?

MACON: Bad boy.

DANA: How come I let y'talk to me like a dog?

MACON: Cause I let y'fuck me like one.

(He chomps onto the burger.)

MACON: Fingers!

DANA: Ohp. Sorry!

MACON: Ohp. Yer drippin' all down m'leg.

(He goes to kiss her.)

MACON: No.

(She kisses him.)

DANA: *(Chewing.)* We taste like Wendy's. *(Beat.)* Yer never normally off tonight.

MACON: Cuttin' back shifts. I don't wanna talk about—

DANA: Why? Place is always hoppin'. Parkin' lot's always full. Alla 'em new girls everyone's talkin' about on the—Two years and three months.

MACON: What?

DANA: That we've been doin' this.

MACON: I know. And now we're gonna do that—

DANA: You ready?

MACON: Are you?

DANA: Friday.

MACON: Fuckin' Friday. Byebye time.

DANA: I wanna grab you. Grab my check. And let go.

MACON: Mmhmm.

DANA: We're gonna need it.

MACON: Yeah...

DANA: Ain't gonna hurt my feelings. You?

(She shakes her head. They wrap around each other. She tosses the burger over her shoulder. Kiss.)

DANA: That was real good.

MACON: Yeah it was—

DANA: Mind blowin'.

MACON: Y'gotta endless tank-a-gas.

DANA: *(Turns on the television.)* There's Evelyn. Category three. See?

MACON: Thank god. Hopefully that windy bitch'll sweep through here and tear the roof off this place. Make this easier. I don't mean that.

DANA: Doubt that. We're snug in the sweet spot. Always turns, tilts, then tears apart some poor fishin' town. Like McClellanville durin' Hugo. Hurricane ain't never been nothin' but leaves in the yard in Conway.

MACON: *(In the mirror.)* Imma do a face mask. Iron out these wrinkles.

DANA: I like 'em.

MACON: Y'see 'em?

DANA: —What wrinkles?

MACON: Fuck you, funny boy. Y'got all them youngin's yappin' at yer heels.

DANA: Y'know that ain't me.

MACON: Ain't it.

DANA: I like 'em strong—

MACON: —check—

DANA: —mean—

MACON: —grrr—

DANA: —experience—

MACON: —huh—?

DANA: —sturdy—

MACON: Fuck y'call me?

DANA: See? Mean.

(They play fight.)

MACON: I am SO mean!

(He ropes her in and kisses her neck.)

MACON: God. You. Say, Dana?

DANA: *(Still kissing.)* Say what, Macon?

MACON: Think y'could get me a gun?

DANA: *(Stops.)* For?

MACON: Oh. Hold it. Wrap my hands around it. Know it's there.

DANA: I can't think up a scarier thing. How about we git ya a bendy straw s'y'can blow spit wads in church? Hey. Lookit me. Y'in there?

MACON: Maybe we could head on over to yer place 'n shoot out the windows? C02 tank? Bazooka?

DANA: Fuckin' turn me on talkin' that way. 'Cha need with a gun?

MACON: It's like all them summers back when we was lifeguardin' at the pier. Gettin' stoned. Climb up on top of the hotel? Toes hangin' over the ledge? Not afraid of fallin', just scared of jumpin'? *(Finger gun.)* Bang! Bang! BANG BANG BANG BANG BANG!

(He goes. She fades back and disappears.)

SCENE 2

(We are now in another space with DANA *turning to see* TODD *taking practice swings.)*

DANA: 'Sup?

TODD: 'Sup. Hell you been at, dude?

DANA: Think I'd miss the show? Ready to kick some ass? Crack that ball over the moon?

TODD: Y'know me.

DANA: That was some crazy shit last week. Y'whacked that fucker into the scoreboard we 'bout died. Everyone always wondered why y'never went pro. Farm or somethin'. Even when we was playin' tee-ball ya—

TODD: *(Swings.)* M'knee. Whyn't y'rub it in? Damn. Much as I love a good ass kissin' y'can wipe that lipstick off my dick 'fore we wake up pregnant. Y'good? Everything okay?

DANA: Yeah. Work good?

TODD: Boner givin' joy.

DANA: Y'love drivin' yer ambulance. Don't lie.

TODD: Yeah I love bein' thirty minutes late to a call 'bout a kid belly down in a swimmin' pool.

DANA: Damn. Everything turn out—

TODD: Nope. Yesterday. Fuckin' blast dude.

DANA: Y'alright?

TODD: Yup.

DANA: Hey y'all find Taco?

TODD: Goddamn you just pushin' all the wrong buttons today, budro. This whole you talkin' to me thing'd be a whole bunch better if you didn't. *(Swings.)* Miss him half to death.

DANA: Stretch?

TODD: Yup.

(They sit across from each other, heel to heel, and pull each other forward.)

TODD: Looks like we're in for a tear and torn with this storm.

DANA: I imagine they'll be callin' all cars.

TODD: Mostly...Not me. I'll be off.

DANA: We'll prolly close too.

TODD: Y'mean they're gonna up and close the picture framin' shop in the middle of a hurricane? What'll we all do? *(Pause.)* I'm just playin'. How's Caroline?

DANA: Good. It looks like she might—

TODD: What say this thing hits us. Y'all wanna get stupid?

DANA: Um, if this thing hits us, we was prolly gonna drive to Florence.

TODD: Sounds wild. Lay up in a motel and maybe turn loose in a Cracker Barrel?

DANA: Her momma and daddy's—

TODD: Nah. Fuck all that happy horse shit. They'll be fine. Y'all come on over. You 'n me'll whip out our big dicks and piss backwards into the wind.

DANA: Caroline'll need some talkin' to—

TODD: Come on now. You the man in that shit or you the man in that shit? Tell her. Little Jenga. Make a fort, tell ghost stories. Some high card?

DANA: I don't know 'bout all that—

TODD: Look here. Do I look like I got my askin' face on?

DANA: Macon won't care we come over?

TODD: You know Macon.

DANA: Seems y'all don't get much alone time—

TODD: Exactly. Hell y'all been these days? Ain't seen much-a-y'all—

DANA: Who? Me 'n Caroline?

TODD: Yessir. There's a hole in m'heart where the two-a-y'all used to be—

DANA: What? Nah man, we just been busy with—

TODD: Get the whiskey. I got beer 'n tequila. Dump yer freezer bring all of whatcha got. We git goin' early enough Imma fire that grill up. I got weed in the freezer. *(Swing.)*

DANA: *(Stone. Beat.)*: How in the hell do I dare say no?

TODD: Y'don't.

DANA: Shit. Alright.

TODD: My boy. Miss ya, my man.

DANA: Let's play it by ear. Make sure it hits.

TODD: Trust me. It's gonna hit.

(Swings. They're gone.)

SCENE 3

(DANA and CAROLINE's house. CAROLINE appears messy and on the phone. She is a wreck.)

CAROLINE: You just can't help but do this momma. Every time? Please take it back... I know it's yer right to know but y'just can't go blowin' bubbles... It ain't been three months yet... How many dagone times I gotta tell ya momma? Of course he knows...Yes. He knows. He'd be the only one to... yes. Yes ma'am. He knows. I'm sorry momma... Oh please don't make those sounds. I can't even tell what they mean no more... Yes. Apple juice, milk and a bowl of green every day. No ma'am in the microwave... well I like it squishy. Yeah I was gittin' to that; Dana just called, said Todd invited us over... Yes he's still alive momma... Well of course I'd rather sit at y'alls but... His wife is Macon...Then go on over to Bill and Rosalie's... Momma? I don't like it when y'get all... Hello? Hello? *(Nothing.)* Ok. Bye. *(Hangs up.)*

DANA: *(Enters, limping.)* Hey.

CAROLINE: *(Upright, grinning instantly.)* I want a placenta tree.

DANA: Hell's that?

CAROLINE: It's a tree. When she's born we take the—

DANA: She?

CAROLINE: I know it's a she—I can feel my new best girlfriend growin' inside-a-me.

DANA: —cool—

CAROLINE: When she's born we take that bloody pancake thing and plant a tree in the back over by the swing set. Why y'limpin'?

DANA: Fucked up my leg playin' ball with Todd. We ain't got a swing set, sugar—

CAROLINE: We will when y'build us one now won't we? Then we'll plant a sapling on top of that placenta, then me, you 'n she, the three of us, will grow forever.

DANA: Um. Okay. Yeah. Sure. Fuck it. *(Heads off.)*

CAROLINE: I'm feelin' like I love you. You love me?

DANA: Yeah.

CAROLINE: Dana Baskins you march yer cute butt over here and let me sniff yer face!

DANA: I need to shower.

CAROLINE.: I like yer stinky face and arm pits. Arf, arf, ruff! Come here.

(CAROLINE pulls him in and kisses him.)

CAROLINE: Mmmm. What is that there? *(Sniffs his top lip.)* Smells like cherries and seaweed.

DANA: I dunno.

CAROLINE: Ohhhh....

DANA: Okay. Down girl.

(She whimpers.)

DANA: Good girl.

(She pants.)

DANA: Ha. Yep. Okay. How y'feelin'?

CAROLINE: Can y'grab me a bowl of chocolate, vanilla and strawberry ice cream?

DANA: How's the job hunt goin'?

CAROLINE: *(Patting her belly.)* I already got a job.

(He glares at her. She smiles back.)

CAROLINE: Macon called. She is a TRIP. We was pickin' on you—

DANA: Oh what now?

CAROLINE: Oh stuff. Talkin' 'bout how y'start rubbin' yer chin and flippin' yer wrists when y'think y'got somethin' big and bad to say.

DANA: She said that?

CAROLINE: Still can't tell she likes me or not. We had a little party plannin' talk. She's got ya pegged.

DANA: Right between the eyes?

(TODD and MACON appear in their bedroom. It's almost time for bed. Split scene.)

TODD: Y'go look for Taco today?

CAROLINE: Y'know if they found their dog?

DANA: I dunno. 'Bout time they gave up.

CAROLINE: That hurts m'heart.

MACON: Dinner's in the microwave.

TODD: What'd ya make?

MACON: Cold fried chicken. Green beans. Biscuit.

TODD: If y'ain't anything, yer mind readin' motherfuckin' cook.

CAROLINE: So sad—

MACON: S'that mean?

TODD: Means y'can make a plate—

CAROLINE: That dog was their baby—

TODD: Means y'can cook—*(Goes into the kitchen.)*

DANA: They can get another one—

MACON: *(Rubs her temples.)* Fuckin' headache. Talked to Caroline today—

TODD: What that ole retard have to say?

MACON: *(Lotions her legs.)* She's a sweet kitty. Y'should be nicer about her.

CAROLINE: We goin' over there?

TODD: They comin' over here?

DANA: Seems it.

MACON: Yessir.

TODD/CAROLINE: Good.

CAROLINE: We gotta bring whiskey, flashlights, extra batteries, and water.

◯

DANA: They can't fill the tub?

CAROLINE: Fer drinkin'.

DANA: We'd just boil it with bleach. It ain't gonna get all third world.

CAROLINE: Just—She said Skippy can come too...

DANA: Awesome.

(TODD re-emerges wiping his chin, gnawing on a large fried chicken leg. CAROLINE *dims the lights and motions to* DANA *to sit with her. She climbs in between his legs.)*

TODD: Why ain't you workin' tonight?

MACON: They took me off the schedule—

TODD: Fuck for?

MACON: Daryl put me in non—smokin', told him to go fuck himself, s'he told me to go fuck myself.

TODD: Son-of-a-bitch.

MACON: Baby don't do nothin' wacky.

TODD: Last thing Imma do is nothin'. OH. It's gonna get wacky. Imma plop that glass eye outta his ugly fuckin' skull.

MACON: Says he wants them younger girls up front on sports nights, like Jewel 'n Riley 'n Lexl—

TODD: Oh please, yer ten times hotter than anyone in that fuckin' cherub choir. All that money we spent fixin' yer beak and titties.

MACON: Cool it. I can handle m'shit—

TODD: Oh can ya?

MACON: —this don't need yer ass buttin' in to make it—

TODD: *(Heads for the door.)* I'm goin' over there right now 'n let him—

MACON: NO YER NOT! Cause that always does so much good? It'll all blow over and be fine next week—

TODD: Oh? Meanwhile y'just cool yer heels and let the bills stack up? How many times I gotta beg ya? It's never EVER been yer fuckin' fault when it come to anything to do with—

MACON: Pump the brakes! I bring home more 'n a night than you do a whole week, in a third the time. Raise yer hand if y'bought this house! *(Raises her hand.)* My roof, my walls.

Keep flappin' yer trap like I'm yer slave. I remind y'under threat of upcomin' gale winds and rain that there's a dirty pup tent out in the garage with yer name on it. Y'can spend the storm beneath it. Can-a-beanee-weenees. *(Beat.)* Can y'just wipe yer hands and get to bed? I'm done with this.

TODD: Yes ma'am.

(He rips the sheet off the bed and wipes chicken grease off each individual finger before dropping it onto the floor and stomping into the kitchen. She strips the bed and marches the sheets off towards the laundry room; he comes to her, almost as if to apologize.)

MACON: *(In his face, almost calm.)* Yer a fuckin' asshole. *(Goes off.)*

TODD: *(Almost punches something.)* ...goddammit...

(She comes back in, goes to the bedroom, grabs a pillow, goes out to the couch and sits back. Her headache attacks.)

(She goes into the kitchen, past TODD who tries to make eye contact with her, to the refrigerator and pours a glass of cranberry juice. She grabs some aspirin, knocks back a handful and chases them. She leaves the juice on the counter and gets on the couch.)

CAROLINE: Git over here 'n put yer arms around me and yer hands around her—

TODD: 'Mind's me of a time—

MACON: What?

TODD: Nah, m'neighbors forgit it.. I uh... when we was little they had this mean ass dog that used to come after my sister's Schanuzer, Pepsi. Cute dog.

MACON: Cuter 'n Taco?

TODD: Different. Handsome. Made y'feel weird seein' how good lookin' he was. Neighbor's dog started chewin' a hole in Pepsi. Got worse and worse to where y'could pull back on his fur and see the meat on his bones. Dad tried sayin' somethin' but dude's an asshole so that didn't do nothin'. So dad took some five times poison. Whatever eats it dies. Some animal strolls along, eats that guy. He dies. On and on five times over. So dad took some baloney and went out to the porch, slathered a dollop between two pieces. Every time we'd head up the road that fuckin' dog'd come upside the truck yappin' and growlin' his furry fuckin' balls off bitin' at the tires. Next day me 'n dad was drivin' to the store, sure nuff' that fucker comes up, teeth-a-blazin'. Dad slaps that baloney in my hand says, "Toss it out the window, don't lick yer fingers." Shithead jumps up like a Mighty Dog commercial, arcs its back, meat lands in his mouth. CHOMP.

MACON: Serious?

TODD: *(Nods.)* Hell yeah. Eight years old. I learned alot that day.

MACON: What'd the neighbor say?

TODD: "Y'all seen m'dog?" Dad shrugged all dumb—said we'd keep an eye out. Prolly ran all quick and hid. Gaggin' and chokin' not wantin' to look weak to other animals—laid down dead. Then somethin' bigger came along, so on and so on...five times over. Ain't even the worse part. Mom was raisin' toy poodles. Had this stud named Rambo. Sold 'em in the paper. When dad made the snack some of that five times musta slid through the porch cracks—Next day me 'n dad was watchin' the game, mom comes bargin' in with two lifeless ass poodles, bug eyed, tongues curled, screamin' "What did you do Jack? WHAT DID YOU DO!?"

MACON: What he say?

TODD: Dad? Nothin'. He just cracked a beer and went to bed without brushin' his teeth.

MACON: C'mere'. Lookit me.

TODD: I see ya.

MACON: Do you?

(CAROLINE *jolts awake from a nightmare.* DANA *reins her in.)*

TODD: S'wrong with you?

MACON: Nothin'.

CAROLINE: Oh. I'm sorry, Bunny, there was a dream.

TODD : What. Don't go talkin' in riddles. Fuckin' turns my hat around backward you do that shit. It's worse than a crossword puzzle. What?

MACON: Scratch m'back? Do that thing you used to do. With that joke about Grandma.

TODD: Huh?

(TODD *and* MACON *look at each other, then away.)*

DANA: You were gnashin' yer teeth—

CAROLINE: They're all wiggly. Mouth tastes like metal—

DANA: Here. *(Gets up to go.)* Let's get y'swishin' some hot water.

CAROLINE: NO...please?

(He stays.)

CAROLINE: Bad, bad, bad, bad, bad dream—

DANA: Felt it—

CAROLINE: Y'think Barrie's okay?

DANA: Is that her name?

CAROLINE: Y'like it?

DANA: I don't like the name yet, but I love her already. She'll get used to yer dreams.

SCENE 4

(A beeping sound comes in as the lights crossfade to reveal MACON *standing at a checkout counter at the grocery store with a full shopping cart reading a magazine. Seal's "Kiss From A Rose" plays.* TABBY, *the young cashier is scanning her groceries and bagging them.)*

TABBY: Y'seen the freezer aisle? All products buy one get one.

MACON: I'm good.

TABBY: Hot Pockets.

MACON: 'K.

TABBY: White Castles.

MACON: Alright.

TABBY: Flintstone push-up pops.

(Bubble. Nothing but a stare from MACON.*)*

TABBY: Y'look like y'like to save money. *(Scans a case of beer.)* ID?

MACON: Girl after my own heart.

(She pulls out her I.D. and hands it to her. TABBY *smiles.)*

MACON: What?

TABBY: Wasn't thinkin' that'd be the year.

MACON: What year was you thinkin' it'd be?

TABBY: Lotta beer.

MACON: Mouths to fill.

TABBY: I wish we'd get a tornado. When I was little at school and we'd have a fire drill or something, I'd pray it was real.

MACON: I like my house. I think I'll keep it.

◯

TABBY: House? Condo? Or trailer?

MACON: House.

TABBY: Where is it?

MACON: Smack dab in the middle of Conway.

TABBY: Fancy. *(Bubble.)*

MACON: Y'can see the river from my mailbox.

TABBY: *(Holds up a box of tampons.)* Ohp.

MACON: What?

TABBY: Y'still need these?

MACON: What?

TABBY: I just figured lookin' at yer birthday that they weren't somethin' you'd—

MACON: Alright sister. Whyn't you just bag m'shit so I can git on outta yer scrawny ass way—

TABBY: I'm sorry. That was—I'm tired. Xanax's the only thing keepin' me awake right now. Workin' a triple on accident. Makin' me see double. "Beep. Beep. Beep." Irrinoyin'. Wasn't tryin' to be rude. I have a way of sayin' things I should be thinkin' and thinkin' too much about things I should be sayin'—

MACON: I see that. Xanax keeps you awake?

TABBY: Y'wanna talk to my manager if it makes y'feel better? Everyone wants to talk to my manager.

MACON: Y'shouldn't say that.

TABBY: Eh. Customer feels rough and tumble like they stood up for themselves 'n Randy pretends to get mad at me.

MACON: How often?

TABBY: Once or twice a day at least.

MACON: Y'don't get into trouble?

TABBY: He wants to fuck me. It's how he flirts. Helps.

MACON: I know that. You new?

TABBY: I grew up in Fork.

MACON: That's a town?

TABBY: Up under Dillon; blink 'n you'll miss it.

MACON: That where yer spendin' the storm?

TABBY: I seen y'in here a bunch all the time. This is the first time I rang y'up.

MACON: Lucky you.

TABBY: Me 'n all the girls here got favorite customers. Game we play. Give ya a name 'n figure out whatcha do fer work, shit like that.

MACON: What's my name?

TABBY: Shannon.

MACON: What do I do?

TABBY: Y'teach exercise one-on-one.

MACON: Ah. And this guy right behind me loadin' his cart with Mountain Dew?

TABBY: We'll call him Garret. He works for uh, he repairs phone lines—

MACON: Fun game. What about her over there? She a Doris?

TABBY: She is a Doris and don't even get me started on THAT bitch. Imma bet she eats clam salad on her crackers.

MACON: How much is the...?

TABBY: Sixty three eighty three... Sixty three dollars and eighty three pennies.

MACON: *(Digs through her purse.)* Shit. Y'take a check?

TABBY: Sure. 'Cha doin' for the storm? Might go over to uncles near Waccamaw Mobile Park. Tailgate. Shoot guns?

MACON: Do I shoot guns? My husband has borin' huntin' rifles. Tailgatin' outside durin' a hurricane?

TABBY: Hell yeah. Y'know how hurricanes go round here. Long as y'got a good umbrella y'don't even need a raincoat. When them mushrooms kick in we break out the guns and go BUCK!

MACON: Don't make me worry about ya.

TABBY: Yer fuckin' cute. *(Beat.)* Loadin' up on beer, don't tell me y'ain't gonna get dangerous.

MACON: We got a little somethin' goin' on.

◎

TABBY: Little somethin' somethin'—

MACON : What's yer name?

TABBY: Cami Jo. Everyone calls me Tabby.

MACON: Macon.

TABBY: That's so pretty. Sorry I was starin' at ya earlier. Y'just got that thang.

MACON: S'fine. I wish we met sooner. I'd have y'stop on by. Shake things up—*(Starts off.)*

TABBY: I don't got a car.

MACON: Right. Well.

TABBY: Maybe I'll find a ride...

MACON: I mean yeah sweetie, yer welcome to—but don't hurt yerself, it could go haywire out and we're down by the river—If m'arms weren't full I'd write down the address—

TABBY: *(Reads the check.)* Macon Mercer? 112 Laurel St.? Conway SC, 29526?

MACON: *(Pauses)* Yah.

TABBY: Alright then.

MACON: Yooooou git home safe!

TABBY: Alright Ms. Macon.

*(*MACON *leaves.)*

TABBY: Thank ya fer shoppin' at Wilbur's.

(Bubble. Pop. Out.)

SCENE 5

(From the dark we hear a newscast in progress: "...schools were closed earlier today and should be expected to remain closed through Friday. The Red Cross has begun setting up shelters at Dillon, Latta and Marion County Schools. We should have more precise information in the next half hour..." As a hammer pounds, the lights slowly rise to reveal TODD at the top of a ladder, hammering into the ceiling. "Due to the unexpected damage in Florida the governor has called in the National Guard early this morning to urge residents on the ocean side of the intercostal waterway to take necessary measures to ensure safety. You have until 4 a.m. tomorrow morning to evacuate, otherwise they advise you stay put—")

TODD: *(Grabs the remote, turns off the TV.)* Pussies. Everyone. Damn.

(There's a knock on the door.)

TODD: IT'S OPEN!

(The door opens. DANA and CAROLINE, with supplies. CAROLINE holding a small bowl with a fish inside.)

TODD: There's m'intake! Run fer yer lives it's rainin'! Scoot the fuck in here 'fore y'die! *(Jumps off the ladder and lands onto the couch.)*

CAROLINE: Hi!

TODD: Darlin' *(Kisses her.)* Damn y'smell like a fresh shower. This that Skippy I keep hearin' so much about? *(Grabs the bowl. Examines.)* There's a good boy! I'll betcha he's a forward thinker.

DANA: Careful. Damn son, y'start without us?

TODD: Hell yeah. Groceries to the kitchen. I'll drop that shit all over the everywhere. *(Stumbles.)*

DANA: *(To CAROLINE.)* Sugar pie, y'wanna?

TODD: Nah y'got it bubba. Put that shit up. *(Pause.)* Pretty please?

(DANA goes.)

TODD: Alone at last, alone at last, the times between, they go so fast.

CAROLINE: Hey Todd.

TODD: Yer bunkin' with me. That alright? All logged up and bogged down. On the Titanic. Without a mechanic!

CAROLINE: Dern. Y'did start without us—

TODD: Shhhhhhh.

(He sets down the fishbowl and grabs his iPod. He turns on "Ass Drop" by Wiz Khalifa and launches into a monster lip synch serenade. It can't help but charm the shit out of her. He attempts the worm only to almost break his back.)

CAROLINE: Y'okay?

TODD: Yep. Dammit. Click off my i-Pod.

CAROLINE: *(She does. Applauding.)* That was good! Y'gotta future!

TODD: Help me up.

(She goes over to him and tries. He pulls her down on top of him.)

CAROLINE: Careful, Todd!

DANA: *(Bursts back into the room.)* Goddamn. 'Cha'll up to?

TODD: Musical explorations. Delvin' into the fellowship that is our next few days—

DANA: Let's give it a day. Tops. It'll blow over.

TODD: Y'got somewhere to be?

DANA: Nah man.

TODD: Refugee All Stars! We gotta whole lotta each other headed our way. We came for the shelter and we stay for the mammeries.

CAROLINE: Yer fulla whatever it is yer fulla right now.

TODD: I'm fulla love 'n whiskey and thoughts of alla us bein' a sweet family doin' naked things—

DANA: Dude. Turn it down... Cha doin' up that ladder?

TODD: Figured' it'd be a fine time to git after that roofin' problem.

DANA: I'm tellin' ya; it ain't gonna be that bad—

TODD: You allergic to the news? Shit's like a movie preview fer the scariest shit I never wanna see!

DANA: Y'gonna do this the whole time?

TODD: Awww. I pwomise to behave as long as y'promise to keep actin' like a full-on little bitch. Now git on over frame-boy and lemme see that dick!

DANA: Rather have a dick than be a pussy—

TODD: I deg to biffer! I love ya. Quick kiss. She ain't lookin'—

DANA: Piss on ya—

TODD: Aim fer m'mouth!

(TODD ropes him down to the floor. It's playful then gets a little serious. TODD has DANA pinned and delivers a series of light slaps to his face. DANA gains control and pins him.)

CAROLINE: Something's gonna break! I don't like this!

(They stop.)

TODD: "I don't like this! I don't like this! My names Caroline and I don't like this! Will y'sponsor me in the annual retard run? I promise I'll win a cornflake necklace or somethin'."

(They hop off the floor.)

CAROLINE: Y'okay Dana?

TODD: Gave me a run fer my money. Looks little but he weren't no easy win.

CAROLINE: *(To DANA.)* Best I saw you turned him into puddin'. I might wanna go.

DANA: Right behind ya—

MACON: *(Enters with a tray of Oreos and drops it on the coffee table.)* Hors d'oeuvres?

TODD: The champion! Now entering the ring. Undefeated! Stackin' up at five feet seven and three quarter towering inches and weighin' in at...the PERFECT amount-a-pounds; bringin' the heat, scoopin' up the field mice 'n BOPPIN' 'em on the head! MACON THE HAYMAKER MERCER!!!

MACON: Y'bring in the lawn chairs?

TODD: Fer why?

MACON: *(Smiling.)* Git the fuckin' lawn chairs in the garage. Caroline, take this darlin'.

CAROLINE: Where?

MACON: Yer choice of any flat, available surface.

TODD: *(Pulls out the Jack. Pours two shots.)* Y'all wanna see somethin' cool? *(Slams the shots in one gulp.)*

MACON: Todd?

TODD: *(Pours four shots.)* The word 'chore' is supposed to mean something to me right now—

MACON: Fuckin' hell—

TODD: Spider-doodle, what's in yer craw?

DANA: I can get the chairs. Where am I stowin' em?

TODD: Beneath the Lido deck, up yer butt and around the corner—

MACON: I'll show ya. Right this way Mr. Dana—

TODD: No, no, no, no, no, no—nope he'll stay here and I'll go, me 'n him'll go.

(Everyone is staring at him.)

TODD: One, two, three sober... I'll be good. Come on. Away we go—

◯

(He ushers DANA out.)

MACON : Slide off yer slippers. Stay a while.

CAROLINE: How can I help?

MACON: Wanna have a sip-a-somethin'? Level the playin' field?

CAROLINE : With who? Y'started too?

MACON : Whatcha gitten kitten?

CAROLINE: Whatever—

MACON: I waited for you partner. *(Pours drinks from a pitcher.)* We're a team now wranglin' them two.

CAROLINE: I ain't worried 'bout Dana—

MACON: Sweetie ain't he?

CAROLINE: Angel pangel puddin' pie.

MACON: Todd was a bed-a-roses twenty-two minutes ago. He likes to show off fer Dana. *(Raises her glass.)* To you.

CAROLINE: To YOU.

(Clink.)

CAROLINE: Oh that is YUMMY. Dern.

MACON: I call it a Royal Royale. Lemon juice. Southern Comfort, a lick of bourbon, moonshine, and Kool-Aid to make it purple.

CAROLINE: Goes down like sweet tea. I shouldn't be drinkin' these.

MACON: Oh PLEASE. I've seen y'suck down—'member that time y'leveled that whole pitcher a—

CAROLINE: —mind erasers—

MACON: Y'remember?

CAROLINE: I don't!

(They burst out laughing.)

MACON: Yer funny. Lookit me. So cute.

CAROLINE: Our stuff is goin' in the back bedroom—

MACON: Arms out like Christ!

(CAROLINE *pops her arms out as if on a crucifix.*)

MACON: That body. Holy moly—

CAROLINE: Yer body.

MACON: Yer sweet. I can see how he don't get bored with you.

CAROLINE: *(Stands there trying to escape* MACON*'s gaze.)* Can I put my arms down now?

MACON: Fiiine.

CAROLINE: Why's he always callin' ya 'spider—somethin'?

MACON: Had a pet tarantula.

CAROLINE: Ain't that a drug dealers pet?

MACON: Got bit by a brown recluse when I was a kid.

CAROLINE: They say it's bad luck to kill a spider. *(Pause.)* I brought lemon bars.

MACON: Good. Lemon bars.

CAROLINE: Macon, I—

MACON: How're you and Dana doin'?

CAROLINE: Happy.

MACON: Y'still lookin' fer a new job?

CAROLINE: Sorta. You knew about that?

MACON: Not workin' must be nice.

CAROLINE: He told me there's no rush.

MACON: Must be nice.

CAROLINE: I grow wheatgrass. I got stuff I do.

MACON: Y'rascal. I bet y'git into all kinda trouble when he's not around.

CAROLINE: I wouldn't know trouble if it hopped onto my eyeballs.

MACON: Comes in all shapes and sizes.

CAROLINE: Todd's funny. On a roll.

MACON: Y'want him y'can have him sister.

CAROLINE: I couldn't keep up!

MACON: Sure Dana's enough.

CAROLINE : Everything I need is right there.

MACON: All yer needs bein' met?

CAROLINE: He's a sweet gentleman I uh, oh—. Oh yeah. Between the sheets he's a hero. Lookit you, gittin' all the goods from me!

MACON: It's fun. I always wonder how it is for other people.

CAROLINE: Guess everyone does wonder how the neighbors do it. Friends, friends of friends...

MACON: Family. People's parents. Your own parents with other peoples parents—

CAROLINE: You are bein' gross!

MACON: How often? How much is too much?

CAROLINE: Dern. Yer gonna gimme a headache. Dana and I don't keep score. We just are.

MACON: Me 'n Todd too. We just are.

CAROLINE: Maybe we should switch!

MACON: Wouldn't that be somethin?!

CAROLINE: It would.

MACON: Think y'could even tell the difference?

CAROLINE; What?

(TODD and Dana bust in. They're wet. TODD is standing only with help from DANA.)

DANA: That was harder than I wanted it to be.

MACON: What's with yer friend?

DANA: Y'know this cowboy. Half hour nap 'n he'll be back landin' bullseyes. Miracle-a-science.

MACON: Freak-a-nature.

DANA: Awful. 'Cha girls gabbin' about?

(MACON starts laughing. CAROLINE joins in. It builds.)

(Thunder and lightning erupt and Notorious B.I.G.'s "Would You Die For Me" with Li'l Kim play as the scene changes.)

SCENE 6

(Lights rise to show both couples playing "Don't Break the Ice." DANA and CAROLINE are much more inebriated. TODD has sobered up a bit and is hammering at the game board.)

TODD: See that? Steady hand and a master plan.

CAROLINE: Oh no I am so bad at this. *(Pulls the piece and sets it on top.)*

DANA/MACON/TODD: WHOA!!!

CAROLINE: —yes—

TODD: Atta girl.

MACON: She's on the other fuckin' team.

TODD: I root fer the underdog. A winner ain't a winner that was never a loser.

MACON: I like that. Come here. *(Kisses him.)*

TODD: These lemon bars are the SHIT!

CAROLINE: Really? You like 'em?

TODD: *(Mouth full.)* Oh, fuck yeah.

DANA: Go Macon—

MACON: Piece-a-cake. *(Aims for the center.)*

DANA: Dare-devil.

MACON: It's all in the wrist, all in the wrist. *(Hits it and it collapses.)*

TODD/DANA/CAROLINE: NOOOOOO!!!!

TODD: Tied! Two and two!

(TODD puts DANA in a headlock and gives him a severe noogie. DANA pours TODD and MACON shots.)

TODD: Still gotcha on the run mother fucker! Cha gonna do mother fucker, cha gonna do?

DANA: Damn y'got m'number tonight. Drink!

TODD: Bubby y'know I'm just playin'. *(Messes DANA's hair and kisses his forehead.)* You know I wub woo.

DANA: Thank god.

CAROLINE: I am havin' so much fun!.

TODD: It's that weed.

DANA: She don't normally smoke—

TODD: I see that.

DANA: She shouldn't—

MACON: Where's she gotta be?

DANA: Lookit her. All fucked up.

(CAROLINE hangs her head and becomes darkly aware of the negative attention.)

MACON: Twisted ain't ya kiddo?

(She shoots DANA a look TODD catches it before she drops in to Li'll Kim's verse of the song. DANA notices CAROLINE watching MACON perform, leering at her.)

DANA: Sugar pie? Sit up—baby y'alright?

(She brushes him off.)

DANA: Git ya some water—

(She half shoves him. He recoils before she threatens.)

CAROLINE: Oh I'll be a child...

(Everyone pauses, startled. Lightning spider legs outside as CAROLINE drifts to the window.)

CAROLINE: So pretty.

("Coolie High" by Camp Lo hums in the background. They all stare out the window as patterns of purple, blue and white stab the night sky.)

MACON: Todd? Yer thick skull eat yer little brain? Y'not gonna tape the front door of all damn things?

CAROLINE: I'll help.

(Everyone laughs. TODD goes out to the garage. DANA goes over to the couch and begins to pass out.)

MACON: He's got it. Come here and sit.

CAROLINE: *(Obeying.)* M'cheeks.

MACON: Yer alright.

CAROLINE: Psh. Tore up from the floor up.

MACON: Yer fine.

CAROLINE: Can't feel my cheeks. I feel like Pooch Puppy.

MACON: Who?

CAROLINE: Y'know that movie with the elevator, he was an old cartoon—'going up sthir'.

MACON: Poor thing.

CAROLINE: *(Waving to the fishbowl across the room.)* Hey Skippy! He's over there just workin' it. Little charmer. This reminds me-a-y'alls weddin'. By the Pee Dee River. Such a quiet pretty day. Out on that dock by the campground. People surroundin' with their campers. 'Member that?

MACON: I do.

CAROLINE: And ya did.

(They both crack up.)

CAROLINE: First and last time I seen Todd Mercer without a hat. Y'had that pretty dress. Barefoot on the grass. Fireflies started dancin' then, right as y'said yes, two black clouds came chargin' outta the day and made it all go night. Rain. Everyone huddled up under the cabana eatin' blue crab. I met so many nice people.

(TODD re-enters and turns on the weather update.)

MACON: I remember. My Uncle Bob loved you.

CAROLINE: Cute ole man. That was the first time I met you. I always wanted us to be friends...Yer my friend.

MACON: Yer MY friend.

CAROLINE: Hot lips.

MACON: Mr. Dana sir. I think this little dumplin' wants a kiss.

(She pushes CAROLINE over to DANA.)

TODD: Shhh. *(Turns on the television.)*

(From the TV: "...unexpected winds creating a system south of Hurricane Evelyn have made the past half hour interesting for the low country, south of the North Carolina border. Grant McCoy is on Folley Beach...")

TODD: *(Turns it off.)* Fuck me runnin—

MACON: That ain't good.

○)

TODD: No it ain't.

CAROLINE: We're like a buncha miles away from the ocean.

TODD: Fuck a storm surge. Wind mixes right an army-a-tornado's'll swirl down over our low country asses.

MACON: Where's it now?

TODD: Crawlin' inland in about two hours.

CAROLINE: I'm sleepy.

MACON: I'll put her down. *(To* TODD.*)* Run go grab him one-a-those sandwiches. Wake him up. He might have to do something. Alright now. Bedtime for Bonzo-ette.

CAROLINE: I don't wanna—

MACON: Better now than later—

CAROLINE: Lie down with me?

MACON: Give sleepin' beauty a kiss over there—

(CAROLINE goes over to DANA and falls flat on him, waking him up with kisses and nuzzles. TODD re-emerges with the sandwich on a plate.)

MACON: Alright. That'll do that.

TODD: 'Cha break that up for? We could share this sandwich and watch.

MACON: Imma take her to bed.

TODD: I like that! Both-a-y'all? Take pictures.

(They exit.)

TODD: Y'alright sport?

DANA : There's machine guns in my head.

TODD: Hell yeah, you were on a mission slammin' shots. Ripped out the rug and painted yerself into a corner. Gnaw on that.

DANA: What's it?

TODD: Roasted chimpanzee soup. It's a fuckin' sandwich dude. Eat up.

DANA: Ain't no baloney in there is there?

TODD: Aw shit! Y'remember that?

DANA: "What did you do Jack, what did you do?" That's a good one. Like when my uncle Kit ran over grandmas cat. Kicked in its head. Shallow grave.

TODD: Aw. This is a good one—

DANA: Ole grandmama, settin' on the back porch. Everybody playin' dumb as to where it's at. Outta the blue she pops outta her rocker 'n goes y'all have go to look—

TODD/DANA: "Here comes that puss."

DANA: Everyone starts shittin' bricks, sure nuff, look on top the hill and see this electrocuted lookin' cat, stumblin' down all poetic—like against a red sunset goin, 'meeeeeeeow'. Next mornin'? DEAD.

TODD: I give the cat props fer tryin'.

(A stiff wind kicks the house as the wind howls.)

DANA: Here we go.

TODD: How 'bout you bubby? Everything good?

DANA: I'm fuckin' trashed.

TODD: We gotta steer this ship across the storm.

DANA: I'm sure it'll be fine. What's this place made of?

TODD: Vinyl siding and particle board. We'd be better off in our treehouse in yer dad's backyard. How is he?

DANA: I dunno.

TODD: Y'ain't been up there to see him on the row?

DANA: No sir.

TODD: Y'okay?

DANA: Rollin' with it.

TODD: Where's that litter? Y'all should be poppin' em' out.

DANA: I dunno.

TODD: Do it. Do it now. Be mean to em' so they're smart. Make sure they know more than you so they can pay fer y'to be old.

DANA: Right.

TODD: Yeah. Macon can't have 'em.

◖◗

DANA: I didn't know. Adopt?

TODD: I'm good on that. Watch me settin' there with some genius Chinese baby, scared it can read my mind.

DANA: That'd be how it went.

TODD: I'd want my own. 'Cha think-a-her?

DANA: Macon?

TODD: Yup.

DANA: Shit. Don't matter what I think—

TODD: Yer m'oldest bestest friend. She's m'wife. Matters.

DANA: She's uh, she's a creature man. We all go way back. Fun. Scary smart. Hot. Life of the—

TODD: She's fuckin' someone—

(Beat.)

DANA: NO. Who? Y'think? Who'd have the balls to—She wouldn't.

TODD: Would she?

DANA: Not in a million?

TODD: I dunno. Fucks with me. I stopped doin' blow when I turned—shit y'remember how I was, so I don't get all scare-a-noid bout that sorta shit no more. We hardly fuck anymore 'n when we do her eyes are superglued shut. Fergit it?

DANA: Send it on its way.

TODD: Down the river?

DANA: Hell I'm married. Yer married. Shit comes in waves. Treat it like an adventure man.

TODD: *(Sits with him on the couch.)* Hard to not step out though hunh? *(Beat.)* Look here. Look here at me. *(Stares at him. Long beat.)* Ah.

DANA: What?

TODD: C'mon man. Don't make me douse ya. Category four in the mail. Lookin' at the eye headed our way.

(The house shakes. Lights flutter.)

DANA: —thar she blows—.

TODD: Gobble up that bad boy. Imma getcha coffee.

(He goes into the kitchen. DANA sits staring forward taking bites from the sandwich before he stifles and begins to choke on it. He tries to force it out before falling to his knees as TODD re-enters, unseen behind him. TODD's first instinct sends him forward towards his friend before he pulls back and considers as he goes to the floor before deciding to hang back and watch. Time stands still. Another moment, as DANA turns to see his friend watching him. DANA almost passes out as TODD barrels over.)

TODD: Alright, alright. Come here. I gotcha. *(Performs the Heimlich and ejects the sandwich.)* There we go. Y'alright bubby. M'grandad always said "it ain't a sandwich race."

DANA: ...wrong pipe...

TODD: No shit wrong pipe. Git ready fer worse—yer throat's gonna bruise like a mother fucker.

DANA: I'm sorry.

TODD: What for?

DANA: Huh?

TODD: Whatcha gotta be sorry for?

DANA: Nah. Nothin' man.

(TODD rubs DANA's back and DANA's throat clears and he regains his breath.)

DANA: It just sucks for you. I'm here if y'ever—

TODD: Yeah I ain't seen nothin' or know nothin' for a fact. But I do know when y'known someone fer a long while. When y'can see it in their body 'n read it in the way they hide their eyes. Someone y'really love? Sometimes that's all y'need to know.

DANA: Macon would never ever—

TODD: I ain't talkin' bout her.

(Doorbell. Knocking. MACON charges into the room and looks out the window.)

TODD: Hell's that?

MACON: I don't believe this. *(Opens the door.)*

TABBY: *(Standing there soaking wet.)* Thirteenth time is the charm! Yer neighbors are pissed at you cause of me. Found ya!

MACON: You came.

TABBY: Wouldn't miss it! Let me in? Wet 'n chilly. Shakin' like a dog shittin' razor blades out here.

◎

MACON: What happened to Fork?

TABBY: I figured I'd take you up on the offer. Fuck Fork. Think I wanna die? We was off to Waccamaw remember? Road blocks everywhere. Wasn't gonna chance it with all the shit I got in my girl's car. *(Lets herself in and steps past* MACON *before reaching up her skirt, pulling off her underwear and wringing them out onto the floor.)* Towels? Towels!?

(MACON runs off.)

TABBY: Where's my manners? *(Goes to the front door and opens it.)* COME ON IN! It's cool! *(Goes over and shakes* DANA *and* TODD*'s hands.)* Tabby.

TODD: You are?

TABBY: Friend of Mandy's—

DANA: Macon?

TABBY: Her too.

TODD: Macon!

(The door opens. JADE, *the silent wild type, is shivering in the doorway.)*

TABBY: Boo-ba-loo. Git on in here. Gentleman, shut yer eyes!

(They don't. TABBY *walks* JADE *by the window and strips off her spring dress.)*

TABBY: Y'all this is my girl Jade. Thank me later.

DANA: 'Sup.

JADE: What's up y'all?

TODD: My my...Welcome to the neighborhood.

(MACON returns with a towel.)

TABBY: Imma need somethin' too.

MACON: ...okey doke... *(Goes out again.)*

TABBY: Oh shit! "Don't Break the Ice!" *(Marches over to the game and hammers a piece sending it crashing.)* I fuckin' suck at this game. I brought blow! We do blow here right?

TODD: We could.

DANA: You can?

TODD: Watch me.

TABBY: You'll have to not pay too much mind. Sometimes we blink and we're naked.

DANA: I think that's okay.

MACON: *(Returns.)* Girls? Boys. Boys? Girls.

TABBY: We did that already.

TODD/DANA: Hi.

TODD: The fuck is this?

MACON: I uh...Yer...Um...They're party favors.

TABBY: Eww I love it!

MACON: Girls. Welcome to the hurricane.

(Thunder. Lightning. Lights flicker. Everyone stops. Queens of the Stone Age, "Sick, Sick, Sick" blasts. Blackout.)

SCENE 7

(Cacophony of storm sounds. DANA fills the room with alternative light sources keeping the room fully lit. JADE watches him sipping whiskey. Everyone else has cleared out.)

DANA: Whatcha think, bases covered?

JADE: Bases covered. Light. *(Looks around the quiet empty room.)* Wild party.

DANA: We're pacin' ourselves.

JADE : Right.

(She dances for herself with a wild and free gracefulenss for a few moments. He watches her. She winks at him.)

DANA: Do I know you from somewhere?

JADE: Not unless y'spend time at the Pink Pony.

DANA: Oh. Oh! Okay.

JADE: Six days a week. Gotta make that money. Chu do?

DANA: I make picture frames. We do custom ...it's...

JADE: Interesting.

DANA: Not really—

○)

JADE: Cool house.

DANA: Is it?

JADE: Gets the job done?

DANA: Oh, no it ain't mine—it's ah—

(JADE interrupts him by sounding out "Row Row Row Your Boat," and leaps around the room. Stopping over him.)

DANA: Little music? Okay.

(In an instant she springs onto the kitchen counter and holds a pose. He gives stagnant applause.)

JADE: Thank you, thank you— *(Slams her whiskey and puts it down. Smiles at him.)* What?

DANA: Nothin—

(She looks for a place to put her glass, she holds up the glass.)

DANA: Anywhere. When I was growin' up we—

JADE: *(Burns her foot on the stove.)* DAMN! *(Smiles, shaking the pain.)* Ow.

DANA: That's on? (*Rushes over and turns off the stove.)*

(She shakes her foot profusely.)

DANA: Y'alright— *(Blows on her toes.)*

JADE: —yeah it—

DANA: *(Opens freezer.)* —ice or— *(Grabs a couple ice cubes in a towel and presses them to her foot.)* Here.

JADE: Thank you.

DANA: Y'alright?

JADE: Yeah. It's like gettin' a tattoo that sneaks up.

DANA: Y'got tattoos?

JADE: Y'can't seem em' but—

DANA: Oh, I mean—

JADE: One big one. Right here. Wraps around. *(Indicates the space between her upper thigh and waist.)*

DANA: What is it? Snake?

JADE: No it's not a snake dude. It's a buncha tiny little people—flyin' a kite. *(Pulls up her shirt to show him.)* Over here and the string goes all the way over here like it's gonna go up and up and up. There's rain comin' down too. When it hits the ground it starts turnin' into flowers.

DANA: You come up with that?

(She smiles and nods. They share silence.)

DANA: You wanna do a shot?

JADE: I'd love to.

DANA: *(Pours them two shots.)* Y'want a Swiss Cake roll? There's pickles in the—

JADE: I ate. Thank you.

DANA: If you want—there's—

JADE: *(Raising her drink.)* Relax.

DANA: ...right. To that.

JADE: To this.

(They cheers. They drink. They look at each other. She smiles and giggles. He takes her empty shot glass. She wraps her legs around him, pulls him in and kisses his cheek.)

JADE: What a host. Potty?

(He points her off to the bathroom.)

JADE: *(Hops over the counter and goes.)* Don't start without me.

DANA: 'K. *(Stands calmly and sips his drink.)*

(The wind roars. MACON and TODD emerge through the door in rain jackets, dripping wet with flashlights. They both fight against the wind to shut the door.)

DANA: Y'all find Taco?

TODD: Hell yeah we found him. He's in the driveway warmin' up the car! Pack up everyone! We're goin' for a drive!

MACON: No we didn't.

DANA: He's prolly curled up under the house somewhere.

MACON: That's what I said.

DANA: Snug as a bug.

○)

TODD: Yeah.

DANA: Y'want me to go help y'look?

TODD: It'd do no good. My poor little guy's gotta be airborne at this stage in the game. He's a miniature dachshund! Had to drag Macon's ass across the yard!

MACON: He did. Kick off yer galoshes and dry off.

TODD: I want my dog, Macon.

(Lightning crashes. Thunder shakes the house.)

MACON: I know y'do, baby.

TODD: I gotta find him. *(Heads back out.)*

DANA: Hey. Y'alright?

MACON: OH YEAH. When I woke up at the beginning of life I knew that this was what I wanted it to be—

DANA: What's with this house that makes all-a-y'all talk like that?

MACON: Just me and a couple of my closest and couple new friends. Throwin' a party. A-okay.

DANA: A little wind, little rain, then a lifetime of sunshine. Come Friday this'll all be in the rear view.

MACON: "Lifetime of Sunshine?"

DANA: Too much? I caught myself after. That was fuckin' stupid. Come here. Knock me one fer the hell of it.

MACON: Yer tight-ropin' the shark tank—

DANA: I've been achin to kiss you since—

MACON: I don't play this game too close to home—

DANA: Come here—

MACON: Yer fuckin' bent over back in yer rocker if y'think— lookit what you do to me. We're too close. Made all the right moves. You wanna—

(He kisses her. She gets into it.)

JADE: *(Re-appears from the bathroom.)* Y'all are outta toilet paper—

(DANA and MACON swiftly separate, but the damage is done. TABBY comes out wearing MACON's naughty cowgirl outfit.)

TABBY: Rock 'n roll. I look badass.

MACON: Y'coulda just grabbed one-a-my husbands t-shirts.

TABBY: Fuck that. Y'got some cool shit in there.

MACON: I know where and what—don't get crafty.

DANA: No clothes? What's in the bag?

TABBY: Choices.

MACON: Scary.

DANA: Kinda choices?

TABBY: Yeah. Right. *(To* MACON.*)* This one? Yer husband? Funny.

MACON: Oh no he ain't—

TABBY: I brought a puzzle.

MACON: That should be fun to watch.

TABBY: I'm hungry.

MACON: Okay. Jade?

TABBY: She's fine.

MACON: Y'always speak for her?

TABBY: When the shrooms kick in I do. It'd surprise me if she could say three words.

JADE: "Three words."

TABBY: She's off!

DANA: How do you know Macon?

MACON: We met at the—

TABBY: Old friends. Grade school. Tight like that.

*(*CAROLINE *saunters in from the bedroom and heads to the fridge.)*

MACON: Mornin' sunshine!

DANA: She ain't awake.

TABBY: THAT'S cool.

DANA: Couldn't wake her up with pots and pans. She's gonna eat.

◖

TABBY: Eat what?

DANA: I'm hopin' fer food. Last night she took down a whole stick-a-butter. Night before I had to grapple a can-a-Miracle Whip from her.

(Everyone watches. CAROLINE grabs a bowl from the fridge and begins to inhale it.)

TABBY: She got?

MACON: A RAW CHICKEN BREAST.

(TABBY grabs the chicken and shakes her.)

CAROLINE: *(Waking up.)* ...no I said I wear a size 11 shoe.

JADE: I know.

MACON: Imma put you back to bed.

CAROLINE: Where'd you come from?

(TODD re-enters. Wind sucks the door shut.)

TODD: Man alive it's FUCKED UP out there. That live oak's almost done for.

MACON: Y'all keep away from the windows.

TABBY: Let's get puzzled!

TODD: May as well just set there and destroy your face with that shit. Dana'll have that thing finished before you can match up the corners.

TABBY: Ah, I'm pretty good, and I did this one already. Git yer own puzzle 'n we can race—

DANA: I'll help you do it.

TODD: He'll do it for ya. We used to have parties in high school. People'd be all fucked up huffin' glade 'n shit. I'd start runnin' around the room tellin' people he was 'part wizard'—no one'd believe me—

DANA: Stop.

TODD: He'd walk around with a Rubik's cube wearing a Viking helmet then he'd set there and solve that thing in thirty seconds. People got scared as shit!

TABBY: Y'some kinda genius or somethin'?

DANA: No, I'm not.

TODD: Yes, he is. Fourteen-fifty on his S.A.T.'s. State mathletes champion—

TABBY: Shit. Why do I think that's sexy?

TODD: —littlest dick on earth—

DANA: Micro-penis.

TABBY: S'why ain't you workin' for NASA or somethin'? Flyin' space shuttles to the moon and Mars?

DANA: They can't land shuttles on the moon. Mars is—

TODD: NERD ALERT!

TABBY: I've never met smart people—

DANA: It was just school. Young mind. Smoked and drank them skills away with this asshole—

TODD: Yup. Blame ME of all damn people.

TABBY: Fer what?

TODD: So this dude—

DANA: Quit it.

TODD: Ninth grade swear to god, colleges knockin' his door to smithereens—

DANA: No it's not tr—

TODD: Full rides all day. Scratchin' like hounds. Full ride to FSU. Fuckin' Georgia Tech said 'come on dude'. 'Stead he just hung back and didn't take it. Call me selfish, I'm glad he stayed right here.

TABBY: Sure.

TODD: Someone had to take care-a-his momma. Made a man outta him. Had no choice but—

TABBY: The hell happened?

TODD: We'll just say his dad is a "local celebrity"—

MACON: We don't have to talk about that—

TODD: My bad. Yer right.

MACON: We really don't need to talk about that.

DANA: Let's get at that puzzle. Ah. Norman Rockwell.

TABBY: That's Santa Claus stupid.

DANA: Right.

TABBY: Love Santa. I listen to the Christmas station all year. That Rudolph breaks my heart.

(JADE is standing by the front door trying on umbrellas.)

MACON: Jade?

JADE: Hm?

TABBY: Come sit with me.

(JADE goes over and puts her head in TABBY's lap, who strokes her hair. Beat. Booming thunder rolls and curdles to where the power of it encases the house. Calm. Brilliant lightning, earth—splitting thunder. They all look towards the coffee table on the couch. A cocktail cup wobbles, then spills. Long silence.)

MACON: Y'never know do ya?

JADE: Feels like Hugo.

MACON: Y'ain't that old.

JADE: Nineteen-eighty-nine. I was around. McClellanville.

TODD: *(Awestruck.)* Y'was at McClellanville for Hugo?

JADE: Just north-a-Charleston. On top-a-Jeremy's Creek. Came hurdlin' through Puerto Rico. Kept tick-tackin' and pinballin' on its way in. Everyone knew it was gonna hit hard, just where for who. The school was like a slumber party at first. Sleepin' bags, snacks, radios. People laughin'. Early mornin' water started creepin' up underneath the door. Dark water. Got thick and heavy real quick. Ankles, knees, waist. Once or twice you'd feel a fish tickle ya swimmin' by. Daddy put me on a cafeteria stool. Right around that time people weren't laughin' so much no more. They was hollerin' for their lives. Chest high. Then neck high. Daddy and some boys took me and some old man in a wheel chair and stuck us up in the ceilin'. Never forget Geraldine Thornton swimmin' by in that pink hat. 'Mind if I come and drown with y'all?' Daddy and Luther Chestnut found out how to get on top of the roof. For years after he always said he didn't know if was better off inside or out. That's when the eye came over. When that happens the sun comes out and it seems like it's over, only for the worst of it is to come... Sooner or later after hours of cold September hell stopped, the water went back into the ocean. Almost three months to the day later—it snowed on the beach.

(Long Beat. Silence. Jolt. Lightning. Thunder. Zap. The lights go out.)

MACON: Shit.

(Shift.)

SCENE 8

("Christmas Baby Please Come Home" sung by Darlene Love overwhelms the stage lifting us into a dance party. Flashlights and camping lights. Everyone is dancing except TODD *who watches intently from his chair.)*

MACON: *(To* TODD.*)* Hop up! Shake a leg!

TODD: I'm enjoying the show.

MACON: The show wants to enjoy you. Git the fuck up, Mr. Host.

(Attention shifts to JADE *and* TABBY *who are sensually dancing with each other.)*

TODD: Them two girls are givin' me plenty to think about.

MACON: How 'bout y'be the judge?

TODD: Way ahead-a-ya—

MACON: *(Kills the music.)* Welcome to the first annual Hurricane Evelyn Dance Off! Judge Todd?!

CAROLINE/TABBY/JADE: Yay!!!!

TODD: Thank you, thank you. This contest was a tough nut fer me to swallow. The talent up here was just so very varied. Caroline downright damn embarassin' herself lookin' like some lost octopus...

CAROLINE: I'm awful y'all—

TODD: But y'had fun didn't ya?

CAROLINE: Oh my god. Yes.

TODD: And spiderwoman over there. The drunk chaperone at the eighth grade dance...

MACON: That's about right—

CAROLINE: Oh. You were SO GOOD.

TODD: The fuck was you watchin'? Her bow-legged electric slide? Thought she was takin' a shit—

TABBY: STOP. Those hip rolls.

JADE: *(To* DANA.*)* Damn, y'gonna let him crack on yer wife life that?

DANA: Huh?

◯

MACON: His who?

TODD: Yeah. Hold m'hand through this one.

CAROLINE: I'm the wife, thanks.

JADE: No I just saw y'all—Never mind. I'm not even here. Makes sense now. I SAW NOTHING. *(To* TODD.*)* Cool house.

TABBY: Wonderin' what the fuck this set-a-legs'd be doin' with this—...fuck...

(Beat. JADE *starts whistling the theme from "The Pink Panther.")*

TODD: Party game! Y'all wanna crack open an old chestnut from back in the day?

CAROLINE: Who doesn't?

TODD: My turn!

DANA: Don't—

TODD: Y'guessed it! It's time for "High Card!"

MACON: Y'serious, Todd?

TABBY: The fuck is High Card?

MACON: Nooo!

DANA: Caroline don't wanna play that shit—

CAROLINE: How do you know? What is it? What's that all about?

DANA: It gits weird—

TODD: Y'all know how I feel about weird—

TABBY: I wanna play. I LOVE WEIRD!

TODD: Lookit here 'n see that slutty, fuckin' fightin' spirit! *(To* DANA *and* MACON *with subtle, violent authority.)* We're playin'. *(Becomes a kindergarten teacher.)* Let us sit in a circle on the floor. *(Pulls out a deck of cards and begins dealing.)* Here is how the game is played, here's hopin' we all git laid. Listen up first timers; Imma deal some cards. Face down. When them cards are dealt we flip 'em. Two people with the highest cards gotta do somethin' bad together.

TABBY: Sign me up!

TODD: Jade?

(Shakes her head and nods.)

CAROLINE: Oh I dunno.

TODD: Y'been playin' since y'walked in the door. Dealt. Macon and Dana love a good game.

CAROLINE: Dana?

DANA: Ain't no one got a gun to yer head, honey. It's the truth or dare without the questions—

TABBY: I'm so excited! This shit is sexy!

TODD: Turn 'em over on three. Playin' fer smooches. One, two, three...

(They turn over the cards.)

TODD: Ace in yer face!

JADE: *(Holds up a two.)* Two.

TODD: Sad story.

CAROLINE: Ten!

TODD: Like m'odds.

MACON: Jack.

TABBY: Five.

DANA: Fuckin' king—

CAROLINE: So what's that mean?

TODD: It means yer about to see somethin' really fuckin' cool. Git on over her buddy boy. Be glad it ain't the blow job round—

CAROLINE: There's a "blow job round"?

MACON: —kinda wanna see this—

TABBY: Fuckin' A. Two guys kissin'?

CAROLINE: Oh lord. Y'aint really—?

TODD: Notice he ain't said no? Tell ya why? One time we was in high school playin' some hands-a-this 'n—

DANA: Fuck it! Let's git this over with—

TODD: Drag them long balls over here, buddy boy.

CAROLINE: Oh lord! Ew!

(TODD and DANA go towards each other.)

TODD: Fuck've I gotten myself into?

DANA: Y'dealt the deck—

TABBY: This needs coke.

TODD: Takin' me back—

CAROLINE: To what?

TODD: Tongue? No tongue—? Who's leadin'?

CAROLINE: Nooooooo!

TABBY: Can you stop bein' such a fuckin' buzzkill?

MACON: Easy, squirt.

DANA: Y'seem excited.

TODD: Risk versus reward. Sacrifice. There'll be a bigger picture in twenty minutes.

DANA: Shit. What's the time on this?

TODD: Til I'm done with ya—

CAROLINE: Can't y'all just do a quick peck? This is too wild for me.

TABBY: Not me. I'm about to slide right offa m'seat! Kiss him!

CAROLINE: Don't.

(TODD grabs him and kisses him. DANA quickly starts to push back but TODD ropes him in and devours him before allowing DANA to push him away. All the spectators' jaws are dropped.)

CAROLINE: Charades?

TABBY: Lines are ready!

TODD: Yee-haw!

MACON: None fer you, wild man—

DANA: We know what happens—

MACON: We got enough to worry about without you hittin' holes in the wall—

TODD: *(Rips a line.)* Let's deal.

MACON: Great.

TODD: Look alive, kissin' buddy. Git yer toot on—

DANA: Fuck it.

(Snorts. Passes to MACON. *She goes. Then* JADE. *Then passes to* CAROLINE. DANA *tries to stop her as...)*

CAROLINE: Just a tiny touch. I don't wanna feel left out.

MACON: Damage is done. Go on. It ain't gonna snort itself.

TABBY: Like champs. Alla y'all! Fuckin' deal. Go, go, go!

TODD: *(Produces the deck and deals.)* Alright. New cards

DANA: Lemme see that stack?

TODD: Nope.

DANA: Lemme see the last one.

TODD: Wrong again.

DANA: What? Y'usin' a Svengali deck?

TABBY: Fuck is a Svengali deck?

MACON: *(Mocking.)* "Fuck is a Svengali deck?"

TABBY: Fuck you. Like I asked who Mickey the Mouse was—Yer fuckin' with me?

MACON: I LOVE you.

CAROLINE: Mickey THE Mouse? Who calls him that?

DANA: Svengali deck appears to be a regular stack-a-cards. It's a trick deck. Every other card is the SAME card and a shade shorter the the one before it. Point is a trick deck is a fake deck and the one who holds it is the one molds it. Todd?

TODD: NO idea what yer talkin' about—

DANA: First ever game of High Card and every game ever since... Todd's rocked a trick deck. Back in high school? At the Mariner Motel?

TODD: I was finger deep in all the ladies—

DANA: Y'spent years polishin' that act—

TODD: It's basic shit really. I just knew there was a better time to break those tricks out other than workin' at the magic stand at the food court—

◯

CAROLINE: He likes math!

TODD: What's math gotta do with magic?

DANA: Every motherfuckin' thing—

TABBY: Jesus, y'dorks, alright, let's turn these cards.

(TODD *holds up a five. So does* JADE. *He high fives her.*)

TODD: Turn!

TABBY: *(Holds up a five.)* That makes three—

DANA: Two.

MACON: *(Holding up a two.)* Two. Imagine that.

TODD: Wello. Hello! Winner winner chicken dinner. Two fer the price of one? Git on over here girls—

TABBY: Shit me 'n Jade have never—

MACON: I don't believe that fer a second—

TABBY: I swear people think sometimes we're sisters—

(The girls crawl to him.)

TODD: Can we pretend you're sisters—

(JADE *and* TABBY *mount* TODD.)

TABBY: *(To* MACON.*)* Are y'sure this—

JADE: *(To* MACON.*)* I mean're y'sure this is okay?

MACON: Trust me honey, he ain't gonna leave ME for YOU.

(TABBY *dives in kissing* TODD, *the three of them go at it for a while.* CAROLINE *does another line.)*

MACON: Well that was somethin'.

CAROLINE: Dern y'all...fun to watch...deal again...

TODD: *(To* MACON, *smirking.)* Mad?

MACON: Not one bit. Coulda watched that all day.

DANA: That'll be hard to top I think we—

CAROLINE: DEAL 'EM CARDS!

(They all look to see she's ferociously jacked up and horny. They all laugh.)

TODD: Caroline? "Y'stoopid."

DANA: Nah, "Y'stoopid."

MACON: "Alla y'all stoopid."

CAROLINE: Oh no. What?

MACON: Nothin'.

CAROLINE: Play!

(Explosion outside.)

TODD: Bye bye, transformer!

CAROLINE: What's all that mean?

DANA: Oh fuck.

TODD: Young lady, it means we're gonna play the fiddle while the city burns!

DANA: Is there another option? What'll we do? Fuckin' law of averages...

TODD: We're gonna tie the couch pillows together and row, row, row our boat on down the road. I mean, we're pigeon-holed ain't we, big guy? What's the theory, frame boy the fuck boy?

(He almost knocks DANA off his stool. DANA shines his flashlight in TODD's face.)

DANA: What's a theory?

TODD: What I just said.

DANA: Was it? Do you even know what a theory is?

TODD: It's a—a—it's a thought, it's a thing about thinkin' and... when you say that— What're y'doin'?

DANA: Nah. Go on, man. Floor's yours. Class in session. We'll just gather at yer knee and let you tell us all about everything. Please though, don't forget that story about how y'failed third grade because you misspelled towel. Or how y'wore Pull-Ups up through the fourth grade. Which shoulda been fifth grade if we all use some basic arithmetic.

(Everyone laughs.)

TODD: Knock y'into next week—.

MACON: Boys? Fight nice.

CAROLINE: This was supposed to be fun!

TODD: *(Points to the coke.)* Eat yer breakfast!

DANA: Alright, my man. Yer comin' dangerously goddamn close to—

TODD: Close to what? Disrespectin' the boundaries of yer marriage?

DANA: There he is. A visit from the past. Right off the cocaine bench—

TODD: You did it too, bitch!

DANA: Bench. I said BENCH.

TABBY: I have some things to slow y'all down too—

CAROLINE: (Big rail.) Y'all we ain't seen shit. Finish the FUCKING GAME!

(Everyone takes a deep breath and returns to their spot.)

TODD: Who put a nickel in that one? Let's turn 'em—

CAROLINE: No whammies, no whammies, no whammies!

TODD: Turn!

MACON: Four? —seriously, Todd?

TODD: ...s'wrong, Spider?

TABBY: King-a-ling-a-ding-dong!

TODD: Three. Poor me.

(JADE holds up a two and makes a pouty face.)

TODD: Git that buttermilk biscuit butt-a-yers over here Jade in the shade. Let's hit that booger sugar.

(JADE goes over to him, straddles him and they start making out.)

CAROLINE: ACE! ACE! ACE!

TABBY: ...hello...

CAROLINE: Shit. Oh. OH! I ain't never. I can't—*(To DANA.)* Can I?

TABBY: I'll be gentle. I gotcha.

CAROLINE: Baby?

DANA: Go git it if y'want it—

(TABBY *blows out the candles on the table leaving the area barely lit and goes over to* CAROLINE *and gently kisses her. After a moment* CAROLINE *quickly becomes the aggressor.* MACON *has been forced off the couch and onto* DANA's *lap. As the others go at it* MACON *rests her head on* DANA's *shoulder, with everyone else very occupied the embrace grows to where they softly kiss. Suddenly* CAROLINE *busts them with a flashlight.)*

CAROLINE: The hell are y'all doin'?!

TABBY: Who cares?

CAROLINE: TODD? Y'SEE THIS?! THESE TWO? OVER HERE HE'N AND SHE'N?

TABBY: Huh?

TODD: Lookit that—

CAROLINE: They didn't get cards!

DANA: Hold up—

MACON: Caroline honey—

CAROLINE: No! I can't do this. I WON'T BE BISEXUAL! I can't do this so y'all can do that, to be that so— NO! *(Grabs the plate of blow and tosses it all over* MACON *and* DANA.)

MACON: It's not what y'—

CAROLINE: *(Shoves* MACON.) What? What?! Y'think yer hot stuff 'n can just take what's mine? I see how y'laugh at me. All y'all. All these years familiar. Make ole Caroline the ass end of things. I should—

MACON: (Grabs her by the throat and shoves her against the wall.) Should what? Y'think y'fuckin' know karate or somethin'?

(DANA *pulls* MACON *off.* CAROLINE *falls to the ground. She runs into the guest room slamming the door. Thunder. Lightning. Beat.)*

TODD: *(Heads towards* MACON *with wild eyes.)* Well there it is. Y'alls thing were a snake it woulda bit me. Y'all think I been fuckin' stupid. I'm gonna—

MACON: Gonna what? Don't y'dare fuckin' touch me.

(He steps toward her.)

MACON: Let's work on my left this time. My right side grew a little bored-a-yer knuckles—

TABBY: Don't y'do it dude! I saw m'daddy hit my momma and I swear—

MACON: Oh good fer you! Who didn't? Y'want a fuckin' parade float?!

◠

TODD: Keep flappin' yer trap and I'll kick the shit outta yer boyfriend over there!

DANA: Todd, man I know that I—

TODD: Know what? Tons of fun about my wife's pussy? Or is it that I can kick yer faggotty ass apart. Pick one.

DANA: Can y'get quiet? Y'want Caroline to hear this?

MACON: Sure he does.

TABBY: *(Zen-like.)* Y'all. Hey. I got this. In my bag I got supplies. Xanax. Percs. I got you. There's plenty-a calm-down pellets fer all-a-us. That quarter ounce-a-blow went flyin? See I didn't even get mad? Y'can do it too.

MACON: How many people are fuckin' talkin' to you?

TODD: Oh do the world a favor y'dumb bitch and drop fuckin' dead.

DANA: Why's everything gotta be—? Don'tcha see how you push 'n pull and drag alla us—

TODD: Whatcha think-a-them freckles all down the back-a-her leg?

DANA: What?

TODD: Nah. Go on.

DANA: I think they're—

TODD: WHAT?!

DANA: Y'wanna know?

MACON: Dana baby, don't—

TODD: I'm dyin' to. Dana baby—

DANA: I think those freckles're like angels' kisses dropped in a glass-a-milk. That sweat behind her knee smells more like love than yer life with her could ever imagine and every time I FUCK her I get to kiss em' as 'fuck you' knowin' I understand somethin' about her that you don't!

(TODD clocks him to the ground. Everything stops. TODD checks him out.)

TODD: He'll be fine. *(Grabs his raincoat and goes out the door.)*

(TABBY and JADE look around the room as MACON heads back over to the counter and pours herself a long stiff drink. TABBY nudges JADE and the two of them begin to clean up the cards.)

MACON: ...y'all don't need to... fuckin' stop pickin' up. 'K? *(Houses her drink, all but hitting her head on the counter, she's almost in half.)*

(JADE *goes to the window.*)

MACON: ...git away from there!

(JADE *steps away from the window.*)

MACON: FUCK. ME. Can anybody in this stupid house do anything I want without makin' me into a goddamn bitch?!

JADE: Ain't nobody makin' you do nothin'—

MACON: What'd you fuckin' say to me?

TABBY: —okay—

MACON: Do I have to spend the WHOLE NIGHT fuckin' people up?

TABBY: —easy does it— It's fine. We're here to do whatever.

MACON: *(To JADE.)* What's that mean?

JADE: What it means.

MACON: Can y'talk so I understand?

JADE: That's on you.

MACON: You some kinda water-walker?

JADE: I'm just sayin' shit. *(Tiptoes over to the fish bowl and watches Skippy, never taking her focus off him.)*

TABBY: *(Pours herself a drink.)* I hate to keep drinkin' yer vodka.

MACON: ...I'll get over it...

TABBY: *(Slams the drink.)* S'wrong?

MACON: Please.

TABBY: Y'sure I can't do nothin'?

MACON: Dynamite the house.

TABBY: Not yet. Y'all're wild. *(Does a key bump.)* She thinks yer mad at her.

MACON: I don't give a fuck. Jade? She's a grown-ass girl. She knows what she did. It's fine. I'm not mad at you.

JADE: Rock on.

MACON: Fuck is her—

(DANA *rolls over on the couch, moans.*)

TABBY: Yer man clocked him good.

MACON: He'll live.

TABBY: Way he looks at you with them sad eyes. They light up when y'lookit him. Waits fer y'to talk— I watched him. All other times he's just standin' in the rain.

MACON: His daddy fucked his name six ways to Sunday.

TABBY: What's with his daddy?

MACON: Ron Baskins?

TABBY: *(Stabbing motion.)* THE Ron Baskins? That's fucking creepy.

JADE: Kinda shit like that runs in the family. Girl, keep that gun away from him.

TABBY: Right? Holy shit. Ron Baskins.

MACON: What'd you mean?

JADE: Say somethin'?

MACON: "No one's makin' me do nothin'"?

JADE: Are they? Is everyone 'happenin' to you?'

MACON: I'm sorry I was mean to you.

JADE: You wouldn't a been mean if I didn't open my mouth.

MACON: So I do everything that happens to me? What about that force out there? Makin' us hunker down and hide?

TABBY: Who said we had to be in this house?

JADE: Boom.

MACON: Y'really got a gun?

(TABBY *nods.*)

MACON: Let me see it.

(TABBY *shakes her head no.*)

MACON: I don't believe you.

TABBY: It ain't against the law. I could wear it on my hip if I wanted.

MACON: I would.

TABBY: I like to keep it in my bag. With all my other pieces of control.

MACON: It's gettin' cold in here.

JADE: Every time this fish turns around he forgets everything that ever happened. Forever.

(TODD re-enters. Soaking wet carrying a dead dog. They all look at him.)

MACON: ...oh no...Taco

(They all look at him.)

TODD: I don't wanna talk about it.

MACON: Baby I'm—

TODD: Don't. Y'always kicked him off the bed. *(Heads towards to the guest room.)*

MACON: 'Cha goin' in there for?

TODD: Me 'n Caroline 'bout to have a chat.

(MACON plops down. TABBY goes to the window to watch the storm. Lights out on them.)

SCENE 9

(Lights up on TODD staring out the window in the guest room smoking a cigarette. CAROLINE is asleep.)

CAROLINE: (Wakes up.) ...Todd? Hurricane pass?

TODD: Nah.

CAROLINE: Why's yer pilla case bleedin'?

TODD: It's Taco.

CAROLINE: Is he okay???

TODD: I'd say he's banged up. Just wanted to be alone with him fer a minute.

CAROLINE: Y'want me to leave?

TODD: House up the road has a tree goin' straight down the middle of it.

CAROLINE: We'll be fine in here won't we?

○)

TODD: Yeah, we'll be fine in here.

CAROLINE: What's Dana doin'?

TODD: Restin'.

CAROLINE: I'm sorry I pooped the party.

TODD: I'm high and drunk. Lost m'job. Wife's foolin' around. Dead dog. I'm a walkin' country song.

CAROLINE: —country music is beautiful, Todd—

TODD: How 'bout you? Y'beautiful? Sorry I didn't git around to you. I'd always thought I'd need more than a minute to take you over.

(CAROLINE shudders a chill down her spine she can't shake.)

TODD: The hell?

CAROLINE: Oh my god, I feel like yer talkin' in m'ear but yer all the way over there! I remember Dana showed me a picture with some crazy girl he called 'the hot dog girl' who got caught eatin' cat food. He said that was a girl y'used to sleep with. Made me feel weird cause I always thought you was good lookin'— made me wonder how y'could go through with it.

TODD: Cause I'm a man. *(Beat.)* That was Georgia Thomas. Nutty chick. She wasn't never m'girlfriend.

CAROLINE: Y'lost yer job?

TODD: Kid died. I was fuckin' off at Bojangles 'n didn't make it on time. I ain't told Macon yet.

CAROLINE: I lie all the time.

TODD: Do ya?

CAROLINE: Can I tell y'a secret?

TODD: True secret?

CAROLINE: Scout's honor. I told Dana and my Momma I'm pregnant.

TODD: Yer not?

CAROLINE: Nope. Never.

TODD: I want babies. Dana don't.

CAROLINE: Yes he does.

TODD: Y'should know him better than that.

(CAROLINE *goes to the tiny window and looks out. The action in the living room re-appears.*)

CAROLINE: Water's climbin' up the yard.

TODD: Ah huh.

SCENE 10

(DANA *wakes up.* MACON *is facing the door.*)

DANA: Oh shit.

MACON: That happened. You're still here.

DANA: We're still here. This is it. We should go right now.

MACON: You mean that don't you?

DANA: All my heart. I can't imagine bein' somewhere yer not. You know we'll be different...
What is it?

MACON: You know I hate seein' you hurt.

DANA: This is nothin'—I won't be. You don't have to. You know me.

MACON: I do. And you know that we need to be true about this and—

TODD: *(Enters.)* Bad time? Catch up with y'all later? I'll be quiet. *(Goes to the kitchen and
starts cutting an apple as he talks.)* How's that noggin' budro? Glad to see y'up. Hate it
if you was one-a-those dudes, cracked his head, walked around, had some dinner, took
a nap and woke up dead.

(Birds sing. Light casts in.)

TODD: Hear 'em? Lookin' like we dodged a bullet again. Had me worried. *(Beat.)* So. Y'crazy
kids figurin' things out?

MACON: Baby I—

TODD: Yes baby?

DANA: Man, I don't know what to say—

TODD: Man, y'don't have to say nothin. No need to run through this, that, 'n the third. Look
here, y'just did things and I caught an earful.

○)

DANA: Y'don't have to make it this way.

TODD: What 'way' did I make? You saw an openin' and dove right in. My grandaddy said "a lie don't fall outta yer mouth, it lives in yer heart," so I don't wanna hear shit you say. Relax. I already hit ya, s'what's the worst that could go down? Like I'll cry suckin' m'thumb shoutin' "life ain't fair"? I'd wanna think y'know me better than that. I felt this on both-a-y'all fer months. Sheets smellin' like other dude's nuts. *(Offering some apple.)* Wanna share some? What? Yer gonna tell me y'all're in love?

MACON: You know that ain't—

DANA: —I get why it's wrong. I get yer hurt—

TODD: Do ya?

DANA: —y'think this ain't fucked up fer me?

TODD: That takes balls I didn't think you had to slice it like that. Think y'get to run free into the sunset while I sit here and lick my wounds hopin' for a new tomorrow? Tell y'what. We'll come back to that one. Y'ain't even close to seein' why it's fucked up fer me—

DANA: —yes. I do. I know why—

TODD: I know this one here better than the back of my hand. I expect this from her. Lookit her. Y'know what breaks my heart? THAT IT WAS YOU! We all been patient with you! Every time y'walk in a room its like a dead skunk hit the floor and we don't pay the stink any mind... Y'let me down. That 'bright future' we all been cheerin' on and waitin' for while we get to set here and be less. "Some day he's gonna be somethin'." Dude? Yer forty-one. Game over. Thanks fer playin'. Yer all yer ever gonna be and from here on, yer gonna be nothin'. Goodbye.

MACON: *(Gets in* TODD's *face.)* You son of a bitch— why ya didn't even try to—!

TODD: *(Holding back hell.)* I wouldn't be in my face if I was you right now.

DANA: If that's how it's gonna be, that's how it's gonna be. I shoulda considered you. I didn't and it tears me in half. Y'wanna hear me say sorry? If me 'n Macon coulda met on the moon and you'd've never known her, then that'd be what I'd've picked. Lotsa things would love to be undone but can't. So here, right now—

MACON: Wait—

DANA: Whatta we got? Y'may be used to "havin' us around" but I hardly know y'even like us. Much as it's—I'm goin' and she's goin' with me. We been plannin' this, me and her, and I can't expect you to—

TODD: Hey. I don't give a hot goddamn what yer plan is. Here's the maneatin' truth. She don't want ya. Never did. *(He takes her keys and tosses them to her.)* Ain't that right, Spider? *(Nothing.)* And that, my friends, is that.

MACON: —my god! Fuck you, Todd—

TODD: Go on now. Nothin's stoppin' ya.

DANA: Macon, tell him he don't know what he's—

TODD: Y'can't never see when yer beat can ya—

MACON: Been beat? I ain't a win! He let me know that I matter. I want y'to lookit him. Look! The one who knows y'most y'make scared to death of you. What the fuck does that tell you, Todd? Now y'lookit me. All them years. A waste of me. On you! For all my hopin' you'd see me I only got me to blame and I'm ashamed for it. Now fer all yer lightin' the world on fire yer gonna be left with the only one that can stand you. You! Y'think I can't walk outta here on my own? *(To DANA.)* I would have loved to believe in all of it. Ain't nothin' wrong with you. *(To TODD.)* Y'happy, y'sick fuckin' monster? Y'got everything y'came for? See that? That's how a man should be. Yer a goddamn child.

(All three of them look at each other. Beat. TABBY and JADE enter. MACON grabs her purse.)

DANA: Macon. Please, I'm beggin' don't walk—

TABBY: Might be best if we get goin'.

CAROLINE: *(Enters. Bag packed. Coat on.)* We're goin' home. Alla this hollerin' is bad fer the baby. And it's bad fer Skippy.

MACON: ...a baby...? *(Windless she looks to DANA. Heartbroken.)*

TODD: *(Shit-eating grin.)* ...lookit THAT.

DANA: Are you gonna let him—

CAROLINE: Dana? Come ON.

TABBY: *(Off the returning storm, terrified.)* ...y'all, y'all can't go.

JADE: *(Feeling the storm.)* ...no no no no no

(DANA glares at him with animal rage.)

TODD: What? OH. She didn't know?

DANA: *(Charges TODD and wails on him. Sends him to the ground where he kicks him mercilessly.)* You piece-a-shit! I fuckin' hate you! Come on now get up! GET UP! GET UP!

CAROLINE: QUIT IT!

MACON: Get offa him! *(Goes in and tears DANA off. Her keys are knocked loose.)* Dana! *(Pulls him back.)*

TODD: *(From the floor.)* Atta boy...

Ⓒ

MACON: *(Holding DANA's face.)* It's okay. *(Pulls away. Digging through her purse.)* My keys, my keys, my fuckin' keys?

(TABBY picks them up. Thunder and lightning.)

MACON: *(Throws her purse and charges her.)* Give 'em here—

(The sky outside grows black. The storm returns.)

TABBY: I don't think yer goin' anywhere—

MACON: Fuck that. Give 'em here—

TABBY: *(Drops the keys in her own bag.)* It ain't safe.

MACON: If y'don't gimme my keys it—

TABBY: NO.

MACON: *(Attacks TABBY and the bag.)* Gimme my fuckin' keys!

TABBY: Look outside. It's—it ain't safe to try and go out—

DANA: *(Gets in between them and moves TABBY aside trying to stop MACON.)* Macon, y'can't go outside, please, listen to her— it ain't safe!

MACON: Goddammit, I'm leavin' and—

(DANA fights her for the bag.)

MACON: Y'ain't stoppin' me. I'm goin' and all y'all can go to hell!

(BANG. Everyone freezes. MACON pulls away from the bag.)

TABBY: Oh, shit, shit, shit shit shit shit...

TODD: Hell was that?

MACON: Ooof. Ouch. S'okay...

DANA: NO!

TODD: Baby y'alright? *(Moving the bag aside, revealing a bloody wound on her stomach.)*

MACON: Oh.

DANA: Oh no, what the hell happened to you?

MACON: I'm good. Just scared me. I'm good. I don't think it's as bad as it...oof... *(Tries to walk it off.)*

CAROLINE: Macon, y'okay?

MACON: It's okay. Stings but...SHIT. Okay... *(Stumbles.)*

(TODD catches her. DANA tries to take her hands.)

MACON: It's no big deal...I need to...

(They try to pull her to a chair, she pushes them off. They are both at her side, trying to hold her.)

MACON: It's fine, boys... I don't need y'all...

(Wind begins to howl outside. TODD gets up from the floor, his head dripping blood.)

DANA: Fix her man. TODD. DO SOMETHING!

TODD: *(Stumbles to MACON with a dish towel, holding it to her stomach.)* Baby look here...

(Everyone looks on terrified.)

MACON: I got it. I don't need y'all it...it hurts a little but...

TODD: ...just breathe...

MACON: I'm workin' on it...I don't need y'all...I don't need y'all...

TABBY: Y'all? *(Off the window.)* God almighty...

(The sound of the sky exploding approaches outside. No one can move. The house begins to clatter. Triple lightning.)

JADE: *(Goes to the window and softly begins to sing.)* "The itsy bitsy spider ran up the water spout; down came the rain and washed the spider out. Up came the sun and dried up all the rain and the itsy bitsy spider went up the spout again."

(The sound of wood cracking as the wind reaches a deafening roar. Glass shatters.)

(Blackout.)

END OF PLAY

Tomorrow Mourning
by David Thigpen

TOMORROW MOURNING by David Thigpen was first produced as part of Program B in Collective:10 at Paradise Factory in New York City, and premiered September 14, 2016. It was directed by Malindi Fickle. The cast was as follows:

JACKSON RHODES   Kevin Kane

LITTLE DEBBIE   Lacy Marie Meyer

SETTING
A prison visitation room.

For Amanda.

(Lights up. LITTLE DEBBIE is seated in a chair waiting. A loud buzzer sounds and JACKSON RHODES enters in shackles wearing a prison uniform. He smiles at her and takes a seat. Beat.)

JACKSON: You came.

DEBBIE: I'm here.

JACKSON: You look real good.

DEBBIE: Yer thin.

JACKSON: I beat myself in push-up contests every day. Damn. Twenty years?

DEBBIE: How come yer smilin'?

JACKSON: Cause I'm lookin' at ya. I can smell ya. Almost taste ya.

DEBBIE: That's nice.

(Beat.)

JACKSON: How's yer Granny?

DEBBIE: Stroked out.

JACKSON: She know about me?

DEBBIE: She don't seem to know what a glass a water is, Jackson, much less alla this.

JACKSON: Yer good to her aintcha?

DEBBIE: Change her diapers. Fix her hair. Applesauce.

JACKSON: Y'ain't never change. Like Mr. Fuzzy.

DEBBIE: Mr. Fuzzy.

JACKSON: We all made funna ya. Y'kept watch over that little hamster and put that duct tape around his broken little leg. I remember me n' yer brother was off watchin' some Freddy movie and I walked by yer room and y'was readin' that hamster a Berenstain Bears book. Y'had circles under yer eyes, poor thang. Some things y'don't fergit.

DEBBIE: Yeah then y'n'my brother kilt him.

JACKSON: Now I didn't have nothing to do with it.

DEBBIE: Hunh. Showin' mercy?

JACKSON: *(Smirks.)* I wasn't even there. I swear.

DEBBIE: Y'was always there.

(Pause.)

JACKSON: He ask 'bout me?

DEBBIE: No.

JACKSON: He know y'came to see me?

DEBBIE: No.

JACKSON: He say anything 'bout me?

DEBBIE: Nothin' ya'd wanna hear.

JACKSON: Rowdy Roddy. I miss him.

DEBBIE: Yer momma didn't come?

JACKSON: Y'know Dierdre.

DEBBIE: I know Dierdre.

JACKSON: She'd either start blubbering' like a whale or start throwing' things at me screaming' till her eyeballs bleed. I put her on the list. Thing to do.

DEBBIE: Right. Y'eat?

JACKSON: I haven't been. Imma eat tonight. Got two BLT's, strawberry ice cream, can-a-peaches and a sweet tea comin' my way. I been dreamin' on it.

DEBBIE: I wouldn't be able to eat.

JACKSON: After you leave that plate-a-food's everything.

DEBBIE: Y' look good.

○

JACKSON: Now she tells me.

DEBBIE: Y'got that "Capture the Flag" look in yer eye.

JACKSON: What one's that?

DEBBIE: You don't remember playin-?

JACKSON: No I remember the game. I don't remember some kinda good look I had on my face—

DEBBIE: Yes you do!

JACKSON: How would I remember a look in my eye—

DEBBIE: Y'was thirteen or fourteen and y'had that little ole prickly mustache like a Chinese man. I was guardin' the border and I can't remember if you was on the other team or not but W.J. Lester came barrelin' through with the flag and and knocked the wind outta me. I was gasping' for air so hard everyone thought I was laughin' so they laughed right on with me. Y'came over and scooped me and carried me inside.

JACKSON: I knew y'was hurt. I know how y'laugh and I knew y'wasn't laughin'. I got mad at everybody. Shoved Jacob Wallace. Granny sent me home. Didn't know I had a look though.

DEBBIE: Y'did. I had no business playing' with the big kids.

(Beat.)

DEBBIE: Y'scared?

JACKSON: What's say we get married? I got a few more minutes.

(Beat. She breaks up laughing at this. He doesn't but enjoys watching her.)

DEBBIE: Can you imagine?

JACKSON: Imma make y'sign one of them agreements though in case this don't work out.

DEBBIE: Lookit you. Drivin' hard bargains.

JACKSON: Y'ain't gettin' my gold.

(Beat.)

DEBBIE: How come y'can smile?

JACKSON: Yer settin' here, Little—

DEBBIE: I am. Lookit me go. Just settin' my little ass off.

JACKSON: My god I'm glad you stayed sassy. *(Beat.)* I like yer hair.

DEBBIE: I didn't do nothin' special.

JACKSON: Shoooooot. If that ain't a lie I'm a one-legged leprechaun. I can smell all that spray.

DEBBIE: Stop jokin'.

JACKSON: Ok.

DEBBIE: You know I musta wrote you a million times.

JACKSON: I didn't get a one.

DEBBIE: I tore em up 'fore I could finish. I hate ya fer what y' did.

JACKSON: Figured.

DEBBIE: Not for what you did with me. Everyone else does even though I was the one that came sneakin'into yer bottom bunk that night. I just hate ya for whatcha did once y'got here. Killin' that man? Y'had six months left. Y'didn't have to do that.

JACKSON: Everything that happens in here is 'have to'. Y'think we all just live behind bars crackin' our gum, makin' 'choices'?

DEBBIE: Imma go. *(Starts to leave.)*

JACKSON: No! Please. (She stops)

DEBBIE: It's rainin'.

JACKSON: I know.

DEBBIE: If y'didn't do what y'did—

JACKSON: "If 'ifs' and 'buts' were candy and nuts we'd all have a wonderful Christmas." *(Beat.)* Rudolph Tyner's daddy and brother are gonna be here to watch it.

DEBBIE: You come clean with em'? Do that thang yer supposed t'do?

JACKSON: No ma'am.

DEBBIE: Better hurry it up.

JACKSON: I got a good relationship with Jesus. He's in this room right now—

DEBBIE: Surprised to hear y'say that—

JACKSON: He's gonna be holdin' me tonight and carry me on home. We talked about it, me 'n'him, and yer the only one I need to say sorry to.

DEBBIE: I got yer letters. Never opened em'. Figured there'd be no point since I can't talk back at ya.

◯)

JACKSON: Y'should read em'.

DEBBIE: Burned em'. The day I got home from the hospital. Y'know I gotta baby, right?

JACKSON: Dylan. He's three. I heard. Where's his daddy?

DEBBIE: Who cares? That little boy is the lighta my world.

JACKSON: That's nice.

DEBBIE: Curly red hair.

JACKSON: Prolly gets his ass kicked fer that, hunh?

DEBBIE: Hush. Y'need to tell Tyner's family yer sorry fer killin' him.

JACKSON: My buddy Jesus says I don't have to.

DEBBIE: Yer buddy Jesus is wrong.

JACKSON: Y'know Jesus?

DEBBIE: I know y'think he's in this room cause yer hidin' behind him.

JACKSON: I'm goin' alone. I need a friend. See, this ain't about you—

DEBBIE: That's right Jackson. It ain't about me.

JACKSON: Look. Y'was young. Y'want me to tell you I'm sorry? I will I just—

DEBBIE: No I want you to know that I AM! Hush up n' hear me. I know I didn't bring y'those razor blades. And I'm pretty certain I didn't help y'slip into his cell. Pretty sure I didn't guide yer hand to cut his throat in half and I'm pretty damn sure I didn't make y'keep slicin' after him long after he was dead. But I know it's my fault yer in here to begin with.

JACKSON: I don't know what to say.

DEBBIE: Fer once. Thank god.

(JACKSON *smiles. He stands and walks, his shackles shake and jingle. She watches him pace. He mumbles to himself. She watches him for a moment.*)

DEBBIE: Aintcha gonna say— Watchu doin?

JACKSON: *(Stops.)* Petrichor.

DEBBIE: Hell is that?

JACKSON: Mr Saks. Father Sakaloukis. It's John, he's the chaplain. He deals with —this— what I'm doin'— he says we gotta find a word, y'know? One that can bring us to the middle— of ourselves to get ready for it. Didn't make sense at first. He says yer supposed to repeat it to yourself when it gets hard to breathe when yer thinkin' about everything.

He says one guy used the words 'eagle feather'—I said that's two words, sounds like cheatin' and he said that don't matter. Other fella said 'rubber pants.'

DEBBIE: Rubber pants?

JACKSON: Yeah it's fuckin' weird. And it's two words. Saks is real smart with words and I told him to find me the right one. Pertichor. He did good.

DEBBIE: What's it mean?

JACKSON: It's a smell. Y'know when spring mornin' comes fer the first time? That smell-a-. grass. Little bit a dew. Sun bouncin' off it?

DEBBIE: Like a lawnmower?

JACKSON: Before it's even been touched. That fresh smell that says... It screams; like a quiet little whisper that jumps up yer nose and into yer head all fresh and says; 'start'...

DEBBIE: *(Entranced.)* Yeah.

JACKSON: That's petrichor. Makes me feel ok about tomorrow. *(Pause.)* So blah blah flippity flu rubber pants and eagle feathers!

(Beat.)

DEBBIE: Y'need to tell them yer sorry.

JACKSON: Y'know what Tyner did to me?

DEBBIE: And I'd say you got him back. His daddy's still here.

(Beat.)

JACKSON: Here I thought y'was comin' gimme a hug or somethin'.

DEBBIE: They made me sign a bunch paper sayin' I wasn't gonna touch ya.

JACKSON: Thass funny.

(They both chuckle.)

DEBBIE: Let that man go. Even if y'don't mean it.

JACKSON: When I think about you I think about that yellow "Save The Seals" shirt y'always wore. Picture of a seal starin' out with them big ole puppy dog eyes. Them funny bangs.

DEBBIE: Y'always had some dumb bandana on yer head.

JACKSON: *(Pointed.)* Lookit me. Look in my eye.

(DEBBIE does.)

◯

JACKSON: Y'see that?

(DEBBIE *nods. Hypnotized.*)

JACKSON: *(Leans forward.)* Now look again. Y'see that?

DEBBIE: *(Pause.)* I do. I do. I really do.

JACKSON: Good. It's always been there.

(Beat. DEBBIE *quickly puts her purse together.)*

JACKSON: We got more time.

DEBBIE: I don't. It's an hour-forty-five-minute drive. They all think I'm workin'.

JACKSON: Oh, right. *(Stands.)*

DEBBIE: *(Stands.)* Jackson.

JACKSON: Drive careful.

DEBBIE: I take the new roads. It's a zip and a flash.

(Beat. There is nothing to say. They smile at each other. She starts to go.)

DEBBIE: *(Stops.)* Jackson?

JACKSON: Yes ma'am?

DEBBIE: What was it?

JACKSON: Petrichor.

DEBBIE: I like that. *(Turns and quickly goes.)*

(JACKSON *stares out with a strange smile. A wave comes over him.)*

GUARD: *(From off-stage.)* There's no more on yer list, Rhodes. Yer due at the barber shop. Git yer head shaved.

(JACKSON *begins to shake. His smile drains.)*

(Blackout.)

END OF PLAY

In Wake of Yesterday
by David Thigpen

IN WAKE OF YESTERDAY by David Thigpen was first produced as part of Program B in Collective:10 at Paradise Factory in New York City, and premiered September 14, 2016. It was directed by Kevin Kane and David Thigpen. The cast was as follows:

RODDY	Michael Abbott Jr.
TAFFY	Booker Garrett
BRAD	Swann Gruen
DEBBIE	Lacy Marie Meyer
GRANNY	Joan Porter
RANDALL	Brandon T. Snider

SETTING
A small party going seven-hundred and fifty miles an hour. The action surrounds a cardboard table covered in trash, booze, drugs and a homemade gravity bong.

For Uncle Greg

("Kryptonite" by Three Doors Down growls from a crude radio as the lights come up on RODDY seated across from BRAD who is inhaling a whip-it from a balloon. TAFFY is in the middle of the room going down on a lollipop, performing a handstand for RANDALL who explodes in applause once it's complete. GRANNY sits catatonic, with silver fuzzy antenna on her head. The first bits of action and dialogue happen all at once and quickly.)

RANDALL: Dern, Taffy, that is so good!

RODDY: *(To BRAD.)* Them things are gonna pop yer brain—

TAFFY: I know. I love doin' handstands with vodka—

BRAD: *(Giggling high.)* Maybe Imma pop yer brain—

TAFFY: Juss something' I always been able to do—

RODDY: Bet y'got two brain cells left. Yer almost outta those things anyway.

RANDALL: *(Overlapping.)* S'good, s'good, s'good—

BRAD: *(Overlapping.)* This point I'll just switch to the paint can or somethin'.

RANDALL: Y'can do cartwheels 'n thangs too, right?

RODDY: No y'fuckin' idiot— I meant—

TAFFY: Cartwheels, somersaults—

RANDALL: Back handsprings?!

TAFFY: Back handsprings! Backbends!

RODDY: Yeah, sure. Never fuckin' mind. Paint can. Congratulations.

BRAD: It's like it turns yer brain in to a magnet. Ain't got nothin on butane though—

RANDALL: I would juss lose my mind on some gymnastics right now—

TAFFY: All I gotta say is Mary Lou Retton.

RODDY: I outgrew huffin'—

RANDALL: She was SO brave! Do a flip or somethin'—

BRAD: One sniffa the paint can'll make a door look like a bagga Skittles.

TAFFY: Ain't enough room—

RODDY: *(Packing the gravity bong.)* —the hell is Debbie at?

RANDALL: Will y'do one? I'll move stuff. One cartwheel? Please? I gotta see that.

RODDY: She is NOT doing' a fuckin' cartwheel in here.

RANDALL: Oh' c'mon just one!

BRAD: Just one?

TAFFY: Please, baby—

RODDY: Not in here.

RANDALL: Please?

TAFFY: Pretty please?

BRAD: Yeah, damn, she's half naked already just—

RANDALL: She's good at it I bet!

TAFFY: Baby, we'll just go outside—

RODDY: Y'all! SHUT. THE FUCK UP! *(Beat. Kills the music.)* I swear bein' 'round y'all is like doin' somethin' hard or somethin'. Can we all just set around, drink and do our drugs like a buncha goddamn normals? I mean Fuck. I worked five straight damn nights. I come home last night— do I get to go to sleep? No! I do not. I have to party my ASS off—

TAFFY: I'm sorry baby—

RODDY: *(To RANDALL.)* I don't work in a library like some people. *(To TAFFY.)* And I don't work in some damn yogurt place at the food court like others.

(TAFFY hangs her head.)

RODDY: I am pretty much in charge of that whole dick and shit kitchen and that is no short order operation. It's an all-you-can eat motherfuckin' buffet and that shit is non-fuckin' stop!

TAFFY: Sorry baby—

○)

RANDALL: Yeah, me too.

BRAD: Are you really in charge of that kitchen? They pay y'more now?

(Beat.)

RODDY: Sorry y'all. I'm not but— this is a special party right?

BRAD: They better not stop the chair this time. Sick-a-all these false starts.

RANDALL: No, I's just watchin' the news. No appeal. He's done for.

(They all look to RODDY.)

RODDY: Well yee-haw. Go in a pervert, turn right into a murderer. Funny how these things work out. Happy trails motherfucker. *(Raises his glass.)*

BRAD: Here, here.

(They all toast.)

TAFFY: Where IS yer sister?

RANDALL: Workin'.

TAFFY: She should be here. This is all for her. How come she don't never talk about him?

BRAD: The fuck y'know about it, Taffy? Y'been around here maybe ten minutes and the way ole Roddy burns through girls y'maybe got another five.

RODDY: Why'n' the hell y'talkin' to her that way?

BRAD: She don't know. Okay? All I'm sayin's y'was here. Shit he was YER best friend. Randall was here. Little Debbie was here. Granny was here. She wasn't here. She's from goddamned Lake City.

RODDY: Y'serious?

TAFFY: S'okay.

RODDY: Fuck y'thinkin' talkin' to her like that?

TAFFY: Y'all—

BRAD: I don't like it when people just pipe right in—

RANDALL: —oh no—

BRAD: This trash bag don't even know Jackson—

RODDY: First off; dontcha call m'solid gold girl a trash bag. *(Grabs her ass.)* Lookit the shitter on this critter! And B whatcha know about Jackson these days? Y'go to see him and shit?

Send him candy 'n' flowers?

BRAD: Hold yer horses. What he did to Little Debbie makes m'skin crawl. Y'know the only time Imma go near that pervert is to piss on his grave.

RODDY: Atta boy. How long we got?

RANDALL: Five minutes.

(Beat.)

RODDY: *(With anger-bitten sadness.)* Good.

TAFFY: Baby, y'wanna back rub or somethin'?

RODDY: We need to ramp this up. Pick up the pace! I seen bigger parties in a port-a-potty! I want it to start feelin' like rabies in here! *(Pulls TAFFY onto his lap and slugs the whiskey bottle.)*

*(*BRAD *starts crushing empty beer cans.)*

RANDALL: I was hopin' we could slow it down a little. Y'all startin' to scare me a touch. Kinda feel like Imma wet m'pants.

TAFFY: W'can play a game or somethin'?

RODDY: No. Yeah. A game. Lets hook up the fuckin' Nintendo and get us a Duck Hunt tournament goin'! *(Stands up, sending TAFFY to the floor.)* And for those who ain't playin' off at the side, we'll have us a little table where we play Uno n' Operation. A GAME, Taffy?! This ain't that kinda party.

BRAD: No, sir, it ain't that's what I was sayin'.

TAFFY: *(Near tears.)* Baby, I don't know. I'm sorry. Please don't holler at me!

RODDY: Oh baby— *(Grabs TAFFY and kisses her violently.)*

RANDALL: Watchu wantin' to do, Roddy? Four minutes till they do it.

RODDY: I wanna hit somethin'. I wanna punch the world in half. Y'all know? He ain't even dead yet and I know this sure as shit ain't gonna change a fuzzy fuckin' thang. Lookit Granny.

(All of their heads snap toward GRANNY, staring at the TV, light flickering against her face.)

RODDY: Wish I was her. 'What day is it?' 'What year is it?' 'What time does LIFE start?' She's no more here and there than the man in the moon. *(Kisses her cheek.)* God bless ya. I fuckin' love you, Granny!

(Beat. They all look at him.)

RODDY: Y'all? Where's my sister?

TAFFY: Oh, baby doll. *(Runs over and throws her arms around him.)*

RANDALL: He stole me a kaleidoscope.

BRAD: —who?

RODDY: —what the hell?

RANDALL: Jackson. When we was little and at the mall he stole me a kaleidoscope. From K.B. toys. Next to the wacky wall walkers and underneath the silly putty. There was this stupid little kaleidoscope. Cheap one. Colored crystals and a mirror. He knew I wanted it. One day when we was all at the mall when it was brand new, Jackson shoved that kaleidoscope down his pants and and once we was in the parking lot he tapped it into my hand with a little wink and a nod. My eyes got as big as onion rings. Some things y'don't never fergit.

BRAD: Y'all fuck after?

RANDALL: I was tryin' to say somethin' nice. Give a good thought. He IS— he's gonna die here, real soon. I was just thinkin'—

BRAD: *(Pointed attack.)* Y'wish he was yer boyfriend, don't ya?

RANDALL: Scuse me?

BRAD: Yer such a little queer, ain'tcha?

TAFFY: Brad.

BRAD: Nah nah nah nah nah nah nah nah... Just lookit him. Way he talks. Way he walks. Queer as a three dollar bill. How in the hell y'gonna be anything? JUST LOOK ATCHA. It wouldn't surprise me none if ya just took off flyin' round the room!

TAFFY: —Brad—

BRAD: Flappin' yer little wings. *(Parades across the room and places* GRANNY*'s head piece on* RANDALL.*)* How 'bout that? If y'was a cereal you'd be Fruit Loops. Or Queerios. Pour milk on em' and they eat each other. How 'bout that, little Randall? Fancy pants. *(Starts flicking his ear.)* See, ole Roddy here, he'll argue about the time of day 'n the color of night and he ain't said a word. How 'bout that, Gaybo? How 'bout that?

RANDALL: How's about I tie y'up kick ya in the pussy and titty fuck ya? Right here in front of everybody?

(An awestruck pause from the group.)

RODDY: HOLY GOD! *(Falls apart laughing.)*

TAFFY: *(Laughing.)* —oh dern—

*(*BRAD *tears across the room and rips* RANDALL *off his chair, throwing him to the floor.)*

BRAD: Little punk!

(RODDY grabs BRAD who keeps hold on RANDALL.)

RODDY: Drop him! Let go-a my fuckin' cousin 'fore I crack yer skull! Knock y'into next week.

(BRAD drops RANDALL who falls shaking to the floor.)

RODDY: Go 'head! Talk s'more funny shit fore' I make y'see all silver! *(Hurls BRAD across the room, and jumps on top of him.)*

TAFFY: RODDY!!!

RANDALL: S'okay. DON'T!

(Just then, LITTLE DEBBIE enters the trailer. They all stop and look to her. Beat.)

DEBBIE: What I miss?

(RODDY dismounts BRAD.)

RODDY: Kept picturin' you in a ditch. Fuck you been, sissy?

DEBBIE: Work. Like I said.

RODDY: Y'almost missed it.

DEBBIE: Yeah. S'goin' on here?

RODDY: Waitin' on you.

DEBBIE: Messy in here.

TAFFY: Imma clean—

RODDY: Where y'been all day?

DEBBIE: I told you. I been workin'. This whole 'celebration' is yer idea.

RODDY: S'all fer you.

TAFFY: Come on over here 'n' hug m' neck.

(Near tears, DEBBIE obeys reluctantly.)

TAFFY: I'm so sorry, honey.

DEBBIE: I'm fine. I'm fine.

RODDY: Took y'so long, Little?

DEBBIE: Oh I had this table— wouldn't leave— Darryl don't like us to give the— give the check until it—

◯⟩

RANDALL: *(Off the TV.)* There he is!

(They all perk towards the television.)

TAFFY: They already showed that one. That's this mornin'.

BRAD: Lookit him. Shit-eatin' grin. What he did to you.

RODDY: I hope he sizzles when he fries.

(They all stare transfixed at the television. One by one being drawn in further by the newscast. RODDY goes to DEBBIE. Wraps his arms around her.)

RANDALL: They ain't gonna show that. Two minutes.

TAFFY: C'mon, y'all, let's head on out and do them fireworks.

RODDY: Right. Y'all go on.

(After a moment of stillness TAFFY taps BRAD then RANDALL and they follow her out. RODDY stares long and hard at DEBBIE. He goes over and takes her hand. She holds back being near to tears.)

RODDY: Ain't this a good thing?

(DEBBIE sniffs and nods.)

RODDY: Hey. This ain't worth one-a-yer tears.

DEBBIE: I'm fine, Roddy. Go shoot yer fireworks. I'm just tired is all. I'm happy for ya.

RODDY: Happy fer me? Hell this ain't never been about me, Little. It's all about you.

DEBBIE: *(Pointed.)* Is it Roddy? All about me?

RODDY: Hey. What?

DEBBIE: *(Touches his face.)* Y'think he deserves to die fer what happened with me?

RODDY: Y'know what they say about how the Lord works?

DEBBIE: Go shoot yer fireworks. Go celebrate.

(RODDY turns to go.)

DEBBIE: Remember that Halloween? When me you and Jackson was real little and dressed up as Alvin and the Chipmunks?

RODDY: What?

DEBBIE: Two-a-you was always like thunder and lightnin'.

RODDY: *(Kneels in front of her.)* Hunh?

DEBBIE: Yer a big ole brother aintcha?

(Tears dripping; He shoots her the bird.)

RODDY: Yer welcome. *(Walks out proudly.)*

*(*DEBBIE *sits there near to* GRANNY *as the light on the television flickers. From outside we hear:)*

BRAD/RANDALL/TAFFY: THREE, TWO, ONE!

(Sound of fireworks. GRANNY *comes to life. Her catatonic gaze come to life. When she speaks she does so with rust, as if she hasn't spoken in ten years.)*

GRANNY: —it's scary—

DEBBIE: *(Thunderstruck.)* Oh, y'in there Granny?

GRANNY: —how some people feel they don't deserve love. Must be awful. Yer big brother's one a those people. Like his daddy. Y'mad, honey?

DEBBIE: I don't know what I am, Granny—

GRANNY: There's worse things in life than dyin' y'know? Heaven 'n hell ain't no real place. Y'know what honey? It's just what y'leave behind. People love me when I go? Heaven. People hate me? Hell. Ain't no clouds 'n fire. We most of us end up in the middle. You 'n that boy Jackson was cute as kids. I never saw nothin' wrong with it. Yer granddaddy was nine years older 'n me. *(Beat.)* Can you git me some flower pots so I can make flower pot bread for y'all once I can get up outta this chair?

DEBBIE: Of course. I love you, Granny.

(They smile for themselves before GRANNY *is gone.)*

(Blackout.)

END OF PLAY

DAVID THIGPEN

Born and raised in South Carolina. Other plays include *Split Left; Split Right* (co-written with Brock Glor) and *Hogtied*. Short plays include *Turtleface*, *In Wake of Yesterday*, *Tomorrow Mourning*, and *Mariner Motel*. *Turtleface* was produced as an award-winning short film of the same name in 2016 by CollectiveNY Films and is available on Amazon. David is currently developing "BRIDGES"—a psychological adventure television series. He currently resides in Brooklyn.

THE COLLECTIVE NY unites professional artists who share a responsibility to create work in the contemporary American Theatre that is emotionally truthful, socially relevant, and defiantly accessible. The company was established in the tradition of the Group Theatre out of a belief that the current conditions of commercialized theatre necessitate collective action. Commitment to a permanent ensemble distinguishes The Collective. Through a shared vocabulary, uniform technique, and continual practice, the group pursues a common purpose: to establish a theatre that is uncompromising, relevant, and inclusive.

Other publications available from **The Collective NY**:

The Collective:10 Play Anthology
VOLUMES 1-5

THE COLLECTIVE NY

www.thecollective-ny.org